BEAUTIFULLY BROKEN

&

ASTOUNDINGLY WHOLE

Matthew,
· Be brave.
· Bring Light.
· Love more.
Sarah Crossman Sullivan

Throw off the facade of perfection.
Capture the strength of growing
in grit, grace, hope, and love.

Sarah Crossman Sullivan, JD

ISBN: 978-1-7339187-0-1 (Hardcover)
eISBN: 978-1-7339187-2-5 (eBook)
Library of Congress Control Number: 2019909052

While the author has made every effort to provide accurate citation and contact information at the time of publication, neither the publisher, nor printer, nor distributor, nor the author assumes any responsibility for errors, or for changes that occurred after that publication. Further the publisher, printer, distributor, and author do not assume any responsibility for third party websites or their content.

Printed in the United States of America.

N|T NEWTYPE
NEWTYPE Publishing
Redding, CA, USA
newtypepublishing.com

For Chris, Jack, Henry, Cecily, and Gabrielle Joy

CONTENTS

It's time to
awaken the awe
inside you.

CHAPTER ONE

A PRIVILEGE AND AN ADVENTURE

Speak of what you witness. The pains, pardons, and phenomenal joys. Scared or in blissful awe. Take off your shoes and linger on holy ground.

Live a life of exclamation, observation, and restoration, for you are exquisitely welcome in this world.

"What's shaking, chiefy baby?"

It's said this was the customary greeting offered by United States Supreme Court Justice Thurgood Marshall to Chief Justice Warren Burger.

On reverent, marbled walkways or along crumbling, unsteady paths, a smile is a mighty spark. We rekindle the world by lighting one person at a time.

Justice Marshall, the grandson of a slave who became an icon of civil rights and social reform, had a sense of humor and understood *our call for companionship*. This light-bearing pioneer and life-long learner aptly observed how certain people have a way of saying things that shake us at the core. They do, and profound power rests in our reply.

In the midst of our wandering through hallowed halls, perhaps wrestling with darkness, someone brings little pieces of light to rekindle our souls and remind us that life is a wonderful privilege and a grand adventure.

It's time to awaken the awe inside you.

Your whole life is a life worth living.

Here. Now. Us. This is where great wonder resides. Abundance awaits in the present, and yet we tend to long for what is ahead or behind. The quest for wholeness – fullness and meaning - is soul-stirring, awakening us to delight in the day; to be the joy in lowly and lofty places alike; and to become radical listeners who walk in humor and humility with grit, grace, hope, and love. Our constant rush, egos, and fatigue obstruct the ideal. We repeatedly plunge into self-made prisons because we do not repair fresh scratches, unresolved grief, and old wounds.

Sometimes we get so caught up in researching DNA ancestry to connect with our past, we forget to cross the room and heal our present. We go on herculean trips to aid in other lands when people in our city, neighborhood, and family rooms hunger for kinship. Life is an invitation to love. Not just love the ones who smell good and look good. We are called to lavish kindness on the obscure, forsaken, marginalized, confused, wayward, and disagreeable. All of us, for brief, frantic, traffic-filled, coffee ordering moments or enduring generations, share life.

You are a brave peacemaker and noble warrior. You are a formidable force and tender caregiver, for you are alive, and every day you choose to act out of love or fear; out of resurgence or exhaustion; out of mercy or insecurity. We are interwoven, connected people who are not called to unilaterally fit in, but are instead called to grow in grit, grace, hope, and love, through and with unique, special, glorious design.

Seeking wholeness is the grand expression of love. We awaken to the astounding, awe-inspiring life we are born to live. We stop doubting. We come alive.

It's time to crawl out of the hole.

Escape from the lies we let in.

Our minds can become our tomb.

Grit, grace, hope, and love are the keys to breaking free.

A few weeks ago, I had a night we all know well, for I couldn't sleep and began scrolling through news feeds. I saw a report of a rescued cat. The news photo captivated me before the headline did. Somehow this fuzzy creature got herself stuck atop a tall utility pole. She got up but couldn't get down. The image of this cat precariously stranded embodies all of us who have ever muttered to ourselves, "It seemed like a good idea at the time." Calls flooded 911 operators seeking aid for the fragile feline. She perched high above with all four paws clinging for life while waiting for help. Rescue arrived via firefighters who climbed up the live power pole to bring her down to safety. They carried her into the arms of her thankful family. And the story ends. Or perhaps it magnificently begins.

We know what it's like to feel alone, hurting, and even afraid. We see life bounding on while we are saddled with momentary troubles. We miss the way out and then along comes support – a safe landing, a small gesture of kindness, a helping hand - assuring we are not alone.

Cat rescues can only captivate for so long. I couldn't sleep that night because I was sitting beside our oldest son, Jack. He was in the hospital fighting a serious allergic reaction to antibiotics.

He was in pain. I touched his cheek. Held his hand. I got close and whispered, "We're all in this with you. Your dad, me, your brother, and sisters, we love you. It is an honor, joy, and privilege to love you."

He asked about Grace.

She was in a hospital room on the floor above us. Grace was dying.

He didn't know Grace personally; he just knew of her as we'd prayed for her and spoke of her journey. She was a well-loved, well-known child in our community. We never expected to find ourselves in a hospital room nearby. People seldom do.

When Jack was born, researchers wrote of all the exciting dreams for these babies born in the new millennium. We were told the life expectancy for this generation would bump to age 105. On different occasions, I've told our kids that 105 seems a good target age for me as long as I have my teeth, mind, mobility, and a bit of hair.

In this early morning hour, I said, "Jack, sweet Grace is not going home again, but you are, my boy. You'll be going home until you are 105."

"Now, you've got to fight for home."

Those words stayed with me, as if it was a call for myself and not just for my sick child.

"You've got to fight for home."

He did.

He does.

He is home.

Together we found something sacred in the scary. With grit, grace, hope, and love *you* will find sacred in the rough, mundane, and marvelous.

There was a washer and dryer in the hospital. Not cramped in a basement, but on the surgical floor in a kitchen designed for families and caregivers. The hard reality is you and I cannot fix every ache, hurt, and pain. In the middle of the night, a worried parent cannot immediately heal his child's wound, but he can do a load of laundry. He can repair the problem of stinky clothes amassed in a long hospital stay. He can do a healing thing because others first saw the need and provided solutions. Loving acts make us human. An easily accessible kitchen with hot coffee, cups, ice water, and snacks at the ready in the middle of the night let people know someone cares. Small acts, providing a quiet assuring presence, impacting generations to come.

There is a false narrative found in movie depictions of law school students illustrating the bulk of their experience is polishing oration and argumentative skills. In reality, heavy focus is placed on writing persuasive arguments. At my beloved alma mater, we were encouraged to refrain from beginning sentences with small, transitional phrases, such as "but," because some deem them weak segues. There are times when this small word makes a powerful influential distinction, particularly when it is used to delineate a person who makes a poignant, enduring choice.

Centuries carry stories of people who chose to stand, stay, and resolve. In a land north of Jerusalem, there is an account of a woman named Naomi who lost everything – her husband, two sons, food sources, and security. Knowing her lot was likely starvation, isolation, and death, she urged her daughters-in-law to go back to their lands to be with their people. One, named Orpah, understandably went on, bidding goodbye. The other, a young woman named Ruth, would not leave.

Two women who had no power, stature or conceivable hope remained together in a barren plight. Collectively they had nothing. Despite her mother-in-law's persistent pleas to save herself by running to the arms of her birth family, Ruth would not go, and her adamant, gritty decision to stay is recorded by beginning with these two words, "But Ruth…"

Anyone else would go, but Ruth chose to remain, and in doing so changed generations. Her profession of faith and declaration of love begins with beautiful individualism, "But Ruth."

First year law students are often encouraged to debate whether Good Samaritan laws should be enforced. The interrogatories seek insight on if we should have laws in place to encourage assistance for those in peril. Are we obliged to aid or call for help? Are there repercussions for leaving someone to die, offering negligent care, or giving good faith aid at the scene of an accident? Hospitals and places of respite are sometimes named "Good Samaritan," though we might miss the story behind the name.

The parable proceeds with news of a wounded man, beaten and robbed, left unable to speak and near death by the side of a treacherous road. To stop and render aid would put the helper in danger and deem them unclean to conduct their work and support their community and family.

Finally, a fellow comes upon the scene who is considered worthless, derelict by many because of his heritage. The assumption would be that no good could possibly come from his lot, and yet the story shifts from despair to hope with three words, "But the Samaritan..." The seem-ingly least likely lifts up the battered, voiceless stranger, attends to his wounds and carries him to a place of rest and long-term care, paying for his stay and checking on him as he heals.

And so, I say to you and to me for our whole lives, may we claim the incredible power of a small transitional word declaring that we will choose to do the right, audacious thing even when it is scary to do so.

All may plug along in woe, weakness or strife.

But Ruth.

But the Samaritan.

But you.

But me.

We can make an astounding difference for our whole lives. Our choice to love is a choice to heal, revive, and breakthrough.

We are allies, sometimes estranged in barren lands, tethered to a connected band of luminous humanity. We can let compassion and indignation rest in the same heart, making ourselves, others, and situa-tions better with humility and thoughtful listening.

Late at night when I write, I like to wear my dad's old sweatshirt. The sleeves are fraying. Letters once heralding his alma mater are fad-ing. I put it on and am comfortable and comforted. At the end of his life, on dialysis, Dad still viewed his days as a privilege and an adven-ture. Ornery, obstinate, bounding with joy and amazing ideas, faithful, inspirational, tired, gracious, confused – he was all of these and more, and so are we at times, and the greatest way to proceed is with rituals of grit, grace, hope, and love.

Quit waiting for your whole life to unfold. Go live out your joy. It is time for you to discover how capable and wonderful you truly are, whether lighting a candle or lighting a life.

Unsure of where to start? Begin with grit, grace, hope, and love.

On April 26, 1777, a midnight rider alerted militia forces the British were coming. Sixteen-year-old, Sybil Ludington, rode further than Paul Revere to save lives during the Revolutionary War.

Few know her story. Henry Wadsworth Longfellow never wrote of her tale.

He missed the captivating rhythm of her ride.

Sybil used a stick to beat back tree branches, brush, and those who tried to stop her call.

Her impact lives on.

She rode a privilege and an adventure.

Several years ago, a little girl joined a foster family. She suffered horrible abuse at night in her bedroom, and so each evening as her foster mother came into her new, safe, sacred bedroom to read a story, her foster father stayed in the doorway. He stood in that doorway every evening for a year, hearing the stories and goodnight songs. He honored this child, by reclaiming a sanctuary, a holy ground. He saw her as privilege and adventure.

Your whole life is hallowed ground.

Your failures, falls, and missteps are foundations for greater victories beyond your imagination. But you have to get up and ride. Intercede on behalf of others. We espouse principles in heated moments on social media, but people will know us by our daily grit, grace, hope, and love.

By grit, grace, hope, and love we know our whole beautiful selves.

And we are not ashamed by what we see.

There are wonderful works we are all called to do. Let go of limits. Set aside barriers and let's dive in together into glorious, awesome, positive "what if's" for your whole life.

For what if Sally never rode? What if a family never rescued? What if the teacher, parent, caregiver, sister, brother, doctor, solider, pastor, leader, friend, or stranger never offered you a vulnerable space filled with loving compassion? What if you never completed all you are wonderfully called to do?

We'd all miss out on something grand and luminous impacting generations to come.

Do not worry about what you cannot yet see.

Believe in the privilege and adventure of your whole life.

A familiar hymn to people of all sorts of faiths and backgrounds, proclaims "grace will lead us home."

My hope, dear reader, is you will discover how grit, grace, hope, and love will lead you to your beautiful, phenomenal whole life.

Out of absolute darkness, void, stillness, nothing, seeming impossibility - life takes hold.

We gather with gratitude, joy, grumpiness, grumbling, and wonder. We help our neighbors, rolling away stones, sharing meals and time. We separate and bounce back. We miss things. We hurt. We learn. We grow. Together, we find the glorious way.

We see today is wonderful for today we can begin.

CHAPTER TWO

KALEIDOSCOPE

Our youngest races home with an award from school. Beaming with excitement, she hands me the certificate honoring the trait: HIGHLY INQUISITIVE.

As I admire the recognition, she confidently declares, "I'm highly questionable."

Courageous shifts to dubious.

In an instant we miss a revelation. Revelations ignite revolutions. Love is the world's greatest ongoing revolution setting souls free.

For your whole life, you are so loved, and you are enough.

If you go no further than this single line, I want you to know you hold dear a permeating, abiding, unfailing assurance.

You are so loved. Accepting this truth is a revolution of the heart.

This is boundless, soul-thriving love. It is the truth of humankind—the affirmation that you are wonderfully made and worthy. It is not contingent on you becoming more than you already are, and it is not perfected by an ideal selfie. It is not performance-based.

You are on this earth with energy, blood, and oxygen coursing through your body. You are created for love. You are designed to love.

Not just intimacy; a love compelling you to grasp the totality of providence and know you are exceptional, and you are vitally needed in this world.

Not *when* you reach the goal or conquer a dream.

Now. Right now, as you are—in chaos, confusion or joy.

Love, or the absence of it, is at the core of everything. Lies, omissions, rejection, spite, rousing hate—each are typically rooted in pain. There is great temptation for us to tear people apart, particularly in the expediency of posts and texts. Belittling offers a false sense of power. We impulsively fire off cannons when a deep breath and pause will do. If you are on the receiving end of a destructive force, you may question your rare and valuable worth. Don't. Don't get sucked in to their ache.

We're going to muck things up occasionally by mistake, with intention, or with misplaced anger.

The question is: How do we do wrong well?

The answer is: With love.

For when crises and cancers seek to crush our souls, love has a might of its own. We are bound by love's unshakable force.

My dad would often say, "Go for the gusto!" It was a call to capture dreams; to build bridges; and to love. Without love, compassion, and care, we can't fully process our feelings. We block ourselves from meaningful, healthy friendships. We get stuck in a rut of yuck.

Loving people delight in life and find joy in seeing others excel. They are not afraid to encourage the best in people. They do not fear someone else's success. They create wholeness. They are not afraid of tears.

Love is what we should leave behind when we exit a room or conversation.

To become all we are incredibly called to be, we must depend more on love.

We can lean into indignation. We can lean into worry.

But we will miss the miraculous awes.

Above all else, love endures.

For me, soul-thriving love is inherent in my faith. Stephen Hawking, who contended he had no religious beliefs, still found love's awe. He observed, "It would not be much of a universe if it wasn't home to people you love."

Despite differences. Regardless of assets and inequities, we share a common thread of abiding love. Even with bone crushing cruelties, breathtaking kindness encircles humanity. Love is respite and refuge.

We spend so much time knocking around, looking for purpose and meaning when the call for our lives is to love.

Are you thinking, "Wait a minute, Sarah. Have you met my neighbor? My boss? My sister? The gate agent as my flight is delayed another hour?"

It's easier to soak in this certainty when you are on vacation breathing in ocean air while viewing a gorgeous blue sky. Hard to hold as you are swallowed by irritation, frustration or doubt.

Complicated. Elusive. Lost. It's tough to shake off loud opinions predicting what you will never be or one declaring what you shouldn't become. Insecurities run amuck. There are also the goofy mishaps that shouldn't bother us, yet they do. We let them obstruct love's truth.

A few weeks ago, my family and I were finishing lunch at a restaurant. I saw a friend coming in with his family as we were leaving. I stopped to say hello. I don't see this friend often. We chatted while he held his daughter in his arms. She was clutching a teddy bear and dropped it on the ground. I leaned down, picked it up, kept on talking, and handed her the bear. We said goodbye and it wasn't until I headed to the car that I realized my blouse had come half-way unbuttoned during the bear rescue. Four buttons sprang free and so did more of me.

Bra out. Not so loved. Not so worthy.

But I am.

You are.

He is.

They are.

All of us carry a longing for love, dignity, and worth. We seek it, though it is already here.

You are so loved. This should be the triumphant fact for every facet of your day, and believing it is the most powerful thing you can ever do.

Messed-up. Imperfect. Flawed. Just as you are, you are enough.

True, today you are unlikely able to summit a mountainous dream, however, you can begin readying for the climb. Go. Stretch beyond your inward boundaries. Play in the stretch. Stop worrying about failing or falling and focus on becoming. Don't let the world miss out on the wonderfulness inside you – even if your heart is racing and your knees are wobbly.

Wholeness is not dependent on time, circumstance or outcomes. Wholeness rests in how we endure, savor, and experience life.

Go. Start. Become.

Studies are published at rapid rates and their results can fill us with fleeting pride. Headlines captivate with conclusions:

"Being barefoot boosts brain development."

"Women with big butts are smarter and healthier."

"Chocolate and champagne may elevate mood and extend life."

"Nagging mothers raise more successful daughters."

"Going to concerts and running late helps you live longer."

"Posting pictures of food makes it taste better."

Given these determinations, my reply to life is a resounding:

"Okay, I've got this!"

(Except for the food posting. I suppose I'm slacking and lacking there.)

Without digging into methodologies, we accept these affirmations, whether founded or simply fun. Then life sets in.

Calendar overloads. Unending to-dos.

Weight gain. Sleep loss. Comparison.

Rudeness. Snarky texts.

An extended family member faces another crisis.

A friend, a job, a hope doesn't come through.

Accepting you are so loved - no matter ups and downs, acclaims or drains - is the first step to wholeness, awakening the incredible awesomeness inside you. Believing you are so loved helps quash the noise and garbage bombarding your head - and social media feeds.

Love combats the agony of "un."

Love is a beautiful word of life.

You are a beautiful word of life.

Love needs no qualifiers. We add them attempting to contain what cannot be bound.

Unloved. Unworthy. Unfinished.

In one of my father's favorite books about love, I found a slip of paper where he had written: *We know the agony of unfinished things – hovering around like some sort of specter; there, but not completely dealt with.*

We know the agony of unfinished things. A symphony. A work of art. A dream. There are waiting times, when we have no control. The idea - the diagnosis - the answer is not yet formed. Life also brings opportunities to re-do things we thought were complete.

Love brings hope. Carries us to conquer. Empowers us to win in ways we never conceived. It reminds me of a collegiate softball game. Two teams competing in a tense doubleheader. A senior at bat mightily swings and hits it out of the park, a homerun. All she needs to do is round the bases, but an injury makes it impossible. Hopping or walking is excruciating. She can't go on and her team will forfeit the run. Coaches and umpires convene. Then the opposing team does something remarkable. They set aside their egos and carry their opponent around the bases to home. The run counts. The results are far beyond anything on a scoreboard. Valor is the victor.

Love brought this athlete home.

Love brings us home.

Wholeness is a joy-seeking quest to discover what you are running from, to, and why. Love is in motion - even in our stillness, fervent progression, dodging or wandering. Love carries.

Love is our survival and meaning for a whole life.

William Shakespeare declared, "Love is holy." He wrote of glitter and gold, killing all the lawyers, and backlit balconies. Did he tell the greatest love story? Is it yet to unfold? Or it is ongoing and in all of us?

Exhaustion, tears, and loneliness are proofs of life. They signal we are alive. Our transformations begin in giving and receiving care.

How often do we sit at work or at home and consider, *"What is the most loving thing to do?"*

How would putting love first change decisions, outcomes, and attitudes?

Believe in love's capacity. Act on it. When corporate executives declare they achieve success by increasing empathy, respect, and response time, it means they are leading in love. A family, a team, a marriage focused on being people of "Yes!" all thrive in love. This doesn't mean "no" is love's opposition. Rather, it is the choice to begin a hard discussion or a difficult task with believing all that is stunningly possible. Love lets us look at others in their humanness. We see individuals as someone's daughter, someone's son, someone's beloved. The best teams arise when we know as much about each other as human beings as we do about each other's roles. Love shapes how we communicate, collaborate, and achieve.

In the midst of our undoing, love fastens our wholeness – if we let it in.

Love is the revolutionary catalyst for building a whole life.

Love is an underutilized attribute at work offering the most return on investment. Have you ever known a boss who fires an employee in such a way that the individual impacted leaves with gratitude and hope instead of anger and fear? This leader keeps love out front when life gets hard.

Want to radically uptick the chance of your child becoming a happy, content adult? Be a parent who persists in love. Further their meaningful, individual whole lives without constructing a perfected path.

The seminal differentiator for resilient people who flourish and thrive is having a consistent, warm, loving person in their lives.

Your choices shape knights and nations.

The durable power.

Love is a life of beautifully onward.

Sitting beside people. Speaking truths without destroying. Choosing to go and do instead of waiting for instruction. There is beauty in grief, tears, and disappointment, just as there is beauty in awe and wonder. It grows as we gather together and care for each other.

Do you consider love a weakness?

A cry of the needy and whiny?

A tryst?

Or something set aside for faith, family, and close friends?

The boundless, soul-thriving love and worthiness that is true for every one of us are requisites for becoming our most powerful, authentic, wondrous selves.

This isn't fluff. It isn't something we should deny or ignore.

We seek love when we need it most, failing to realize the compelling, formidable strength we can hold every day.

It's easy to love people who warm us.

Love comes less quickly when it seems some lives and deaths get more coverage, compassion, and care. Bad things happen to good people, and good people can do dumb, awful things. We lose our patience. Loving requires learning and practice.

The world is full of loving people. If ever you can't find one, be one. With your spark, more will light come.

We conquer life with love.

Be a lamp, a lifeboat, a ladder. Help someone's soul heal.
Walk out of your house like a shepherd.
- RUMI

Loving oneself is crucial. If we do not love ourselves, how
can we love others?
- DALAI LAMA

When you are kind to others, it not only changes you,
it changes the world.
- HAROLD S. KUSHNER

Love from the center of who you are; don't fake it.
Run for dear life from evil; hold on for dear life to good.
Be good friends who love deeply.
- PAUL'S WRITINGS IN ROMANS 12:9-10

Parents, poets, patriots, prisoners, people at podiums and pulpits, those suffering and conquering, the strangers among us encouraging a smile - all share a unifying core: we conquer life with love. To wield love, you must first accept it. Varied faiths and beliefs shape our walk. I am a minister's daughter. I grew up seeing love's presence in action. Dad helped mend people torn apart in political, financial, and emotional stress with his loving presence. He offered acceptance, respect, and a marvelous laugh. He spoke hard truths against racism and violence. He loved imperfectly.
We all do.

Each of us has the capacity to live a whole life that is a revelation of love. And love becomes radical when you see its grand work coming through others. It is a profound gift to witness someone grow into what they were beautifully born to do. We are all unique. No matter our similarities and shared views, we are all distinctly, gloriously different. We get riled up sometimes. We may be right, or we might be so very tired and worried about other things far beyond this immediate irritation.

I texted my friend Sydney the other day. "I'm so frustrated by incompetency and lack of customer service!"

Sydney lives in another state. She has her own joys and burdens. She stopped whatever she was doing, and replied, "Wait. I'm calling you now."

She listened. She poured on hope. She nudged me onward.

As I thanked her, she closed with a powerful phrase: "We're in this together."

All of us are in this life together, but we don't always love our togetherness. Space is often the loveliest thing needed between people.

Help is on the way.

Love asks, "Are you okay?" And bravely waits for the reply.

Love's restoration begins within.

Believing you are so loved heals scars – the marks left by childhood, a co-worker, a spouse, a friend, a family member, and the ones that are self-inflicted.

Soul-thriving love is what binds us to rally, rescue, and restore when life rattles us.

Maybe you've known this throughout your life. Your mom's hug enveloped you with security from the onset, making you aware, safe, and understanding all would be okay. Maybe you never had this assurance or someone you trusted tried to break your worth and wonder. But your worthiness was never based on someone else's affection or rejection. Trauma tramples. Love heals.

Understanding you are so loved empowers you with the gift to shake and shape the world. You are a conquering warrior and gentle peacemaker the moment you step into this truth.

You are the person for such a time as this.

The whole of you - as you are, where you are - is enough, and you are so loved.

Love is the most powerful force in life and work. Loving decisions build lasting nations and corporate giants. Families break cycles of pain, violence, and neglect through one member claiming love's choice and declaring, "This garbage has to stop!"

Love lets us break free. To flourish or languish seems an easy choice, but thriving wholly and fully requires difficult, bold, wondrous love. Love is easy or can make you nauseous and uncomfortable depending on the room, situation, and recipient.

Love defines us. Love creates enduring legacy.

If it is all this, and more, why do we ignore it, isolate it, and discard it instead of lassoing and utilizing love's full capacity?

Crossing thresholds, we shift from work to life, back and forth. Our hope is to shut down one while entering the other. In hand is the convergent and divergent – a cell phone. We begin work and life calls. We embrace life and work summons.

One of the hardest and least discussed transitions is "entering in and leaving behind." A view of the compartmentalization of me. I walk in the door and the kids deserve my undivided attention. I wrap my arms around them still clasping my phone, vibrating with an urgent need. Urgency is relative, each of us determining the hierarchy and health of replies. I head into work thinking about a child's worry or the important talk my husband and I did not finish. We are supposed to set things aside as we fluctuate among our numerous niches and roles, even though everything intertwines. *Work me* and *home me* should be the *same me*. Shared vulnerabilities and intimacies vary; however, the overarching triumphant connection is choosing love.

Love is the call of life, but sadly we are trained to leave love outside work's door. Love is the vital spark to every worthy gain. Work and home come alive with love. Love's magnificence isn't zapped because you happen to be sitting in a boardroom. Acts and words woven with love are the strongest influencers affecting a family, team, or company. This is not "mushy babying" or an office affair. This is a battle plan for warriors – speak truth in love, with love, blending in laughter, grit, grace, and hope.

Love is not weak. It is the long-tailed, arduous, glorious work of the brave.

Love is our highest and hardest calling.

Beliefs affect every experience. Henri Nouwen aptly described daily ups and downs, "A little criticism makes me angry and a little rejection makes me depressed. A little praise can lift my spirits, and a little success excites me. It takes very little to raise me up or down."

We all know this pattern in varying degrees. Your day is humming along beautifully - affirmation in meetings, goals on track, swipes through social media garner hearts and shares, and then "Wham!" A call or text with a friend goes sideways when she says something off-topic and hurtful. A client asks for your insight and then doesn't like your reply, so he escalates the issue to your boss who does not back your idea. At an event, someone you trusted and admired offers your original ideas as her own. Or you simply screw up. Spill drinks on a date. Send a reply meant for one, to all. Overspend or overshare out of insecurity and envy.

These acts gnaw and gnash. They cut, seep in, and cling tenaciously to our tender spots. We allow them to stick. We forget who we are.

Whenever in despair, go back to this truth - you are so loved and you are enough.

This is what defines you.

Beauty reigns in imperfection. Looking through a kaleidoscope we see breathtaking art lasting only a moment before the next original array takes shape. The word kaleidoscope derives from Greek origins meaning "beautiful form to see." With light, mirrors, and symmetry, ordinary objects, like broken glass, transform into spectacular designs.

You are the kaleidoscope of life, so stunning to behold. You are a beautiful form to see.

Love sees our magnificent, revolutionary truth - we are beautiful-ly broken and astoundingly whole. Love restores fractured shards and transforms polished pieces through persistent turning.

Remember.

Remind others.

For it applies to all.

CHAPTER THREE

YET I

For your whole life –

You are not alone.

You are called to carry.

You are welcome.

Be light. Be bold. Be brave.

Embrace "Yet I"

I. You are not alone.

One of the best things to hear and know is, "Me, too." Two words echoed and the weight of isolating worry subsides. Throughout each day, there are people providing small reminders of kinship.

"Oh, it's not just me. You, too?" This is sacred relief. Prized connection. Everything changes because in that moment we are no longer alone.

You get me. I get you. We are in this together.

Acknowledged without sarcasm and coupled with simple actions, it is an assurance: "I'm here beside you."

One night I was sitting in the hospital by our son Henry's bedside. It was 3:00 am, a few hours after emergency surgery. I closed my eyes trying to rest, although sleep would not come. The door opened, and a nurse entered quietly. She checked Henry's vitals and gently pulled his blanket back to assess bandages and wounds. I caught her eyes briefly to make sure all was okay. My breath came heavy, like my heart and head. Earlier I had encouraged my husband to go home to our other children for a few hours. He did not want to leave us. I understood.

The nurse attended to her patient. I closed my eyes to rest.

Attend. Such a powerful, beautiful word. Attending to others, caring for one another, assuring we are not alone. My tired body wrestled with worry and gratitude as I sat in that small hospital room. And then warmth covered me. A blanket swaddled my whole body. Without a word, my son's nurse covered me with love and assurance. This astounding, quiet caregiver attended to her patient and then attended to me. She intentionally walked in with a warm blanket to ease pain – his and mine. I was dumbfounded by the blessing of this unexpected, small act. She did not ask permission. She acted as she felt led. Perhaps she considered this simple action ordinary. Somewhere, somehow, someone determined parents sitting at hospital bedsides in the middle of night could draw strength, faith, and courage from a warmed blanket. Her purposeful steps, caring for my son and then loving on me, filled my heart. Had she offered the covering in the morning or afternoon I would have respectfully declined. She offered warmth when I did not know I needed it most and when I was most likely to accept it. Without ever speaking a word, she cloaked me with comfort. She gave assurance and grace. It wasn't something I earned; it was something I needed. This nurse let me know we were bound in the business of healing. I wish I could remember her name. She was the essence of love on that lonely night. Her work was grace. I am thankful still.

Your whole life doesn't happen in isolation. We were not meant to do this alone. While Frank Sinatra beautifully sang about doing it "his way," we are all impacted by each other's decisions. In the hospital, awaiting whatever to come, my way was to sit beside our boy. Another way gave me strength beyond expectation. Both were quiet acts in darkness. Together, we shared light.

2. You are called to carry.

What stirs your spirit is integral to what makes you whole. But we don't need one more quip suggesting "just find your passion." Frequently you must do what is right in front of you. "Have to" and "want to" are often at odds. Attitude is an aid or culprit.

To better understand what makes us whole, we need to broaden our "I am" qualifiers. I am a mom. I am a wife. I am a writer. I am a CEO and consultant. I am a friend. I am an attorney. I am an advocate. I am a daughter and sister. I am a person of faith. I am a listener. I am a woman cautiously watching my neck and arms rapidly change while also being somewhat concerned that aging and dark chocolate may cause my chest to envelope into my lap, but not so much as to put the chocolate down. I am a driver of sweaty, smelly, beloved kids to practices. I am a purveyor of joy, impromptu dance moves, and baking pies on Pi day (3.14). I am a social media monitor. I am a frustrated laundress and seamstress, but a strong 11:00 pm problem solver. I am vulnerable, fearless, fragile, and vigilant. I am tired and worried. I am uncertain in a new role. I am resilient. I am a leader and servant.

I am conflicted, particularly when I should go to bed and then choose to watch one more episode. I am warmly cradled at the sight of my family doing simple things together. I am washed with gratitude as we organize, clean, and purge, and then I'm woken from tidy bliss by trying to buy large storage containers with matching lids. With these cumbersome essentials often tucked in the corner of a retail store, far from a coffee counter or employee or emergency call button, it makes heading to the front for purchase a death-defying shopping cart ride.

Some "I am's" are fluid. Others come and hold our hearts forever. They are wonderful, rewarding, and difficult. Intermittently uncomfortable at first. They are parts of the aggregate of me. They are parts of my purpose and what I carry. The same is true for you. There is unrivaled, untapped strength resting within for all you are called to carry.

You and I share "I am's." I am loved. I am able. You are too.

Becoming whole, growing in grit, grace, hope, and love, we learn how to carry each other. The weight of what we hold shifts. Sometimes the load is light, sometimes it is more than we think we can bear. To live a whole life, we carry each other.

We bring restoration and relief.

We elevate this *call* to a *gift* when we view carrying each other as "get to" in lieu of "have to."

"We get to" – with three words, a burden becomes a blessing.

You and I get to live this beautiful, bountiful, barren, burdensome, bubbly life together. We get to be and become. We get to carry each other.

Living a whole life lifts us from indifference to empathy.

When I was twelve, I went on a river tubing trip. Lakes, pools, and an ocean were my earlier experiences and I was excited to discover a new adventure with my youth group. Ranging in age from twelve to seventeen, we drifted down a river, jumping on and off floats to enjoy the rush of diving into cold water. I began exploring on my own and swam to the river bank to view what might lie beneath. Although near the edge, the water was deep. My eyes were focused on what was below me, never looking ahead or above. Admiring fish, I became wickedly entangled in tree roots. My heart raced as I could not figure out how to escape the roots and reach the surface for air. I was not wearing a mask or goggles. I was alone. I had left my group for solitary exploration. As I banged my head, struggling, losing air, I suddenly moved from panic to calm. All stirring and worry left. Soothing waves of tranquility swept over me. I relaxed as I saw light. My frantic struggle gave way to peace and stillness. Suddenly a rush, a whoosh, and a powerful tug shocked my senses. A teenager overhead on the river bank saw me struggling and pulled me out by my hair. I was free. A stranger carried me.

He saw my suffering and struggle, and with all the strength and gumption he had, lifted me to shore. I found my breath and awe.

Daily decisions have generational impact on your whole life.

The way, why, and what we carry will vary. Imagine oxen or horses harnessed to a wagon. We describe them as "pulling the load," when they are actually *pushing* against the yoke to move forward. The yoke binds them together to carry weights far beyond their frames.

At our best, we push each other forward with grit, grace, hope, and love.

We are bound for minutes, mountains, and lifetimes.

District Court Judge Lou Olivera is a Gulf War veteran. One day a decorated, former Green Beret stood before him, charged with lying to the court. Judge Olivera sentenced the former solider and then did something unexpected. He spent the night in the jail cell with him. The judge punished the defendant, and then carried him. Locked up, the two talked and began a relationship. Judge Olivera views his courtroom, staff, and veterans' treatment as part of a family. There are consequences - good and bad, for choices - good and bad. Judge Olivera's courtroom community carries each other.

Through each complicated, delicate, lovely whole life, we carry each other. We do so in ways we do not remember or recognize as significant.

One summer vacation, our youngest spotted a little boy lost in a crowd. In a vast, vaulted room of strangers, she saw him. We were waiting against a railing while her brothers were in the restroom. The little boy's eyes told her he was lost. My daughter tugged my hand and whispered, "Mom, that little boy needs us."

We went over to check on him. He was holding back tears until we asked, "Are you okay?"

"I'm lost. I can't find my mom or dad," he said.

He spoke and his tears flowed.

We took his hand and told him not worry. A teacher soon joined us. She immediately began asking comforting questions. She discovered he was going into second grade. She taught second grade. We got a description of his parents and just as my boys were heading off to find them, they appeared. All were relieved. More tears. Then we were off on our separate ways.

For a brief moment, we carried each other. Strangers became community.

What was lost was found.

In a world with news of hate, violence, and fear, love prevails. It is bigger and more prevalent than any pocket of despair.

We are all children who are loved, but we occasionally get lost.

Becoming whole, carrying each other through life, are delicate, beautiful gifts as we each find our way home.

4. You are welcome.

There is a place and space for you where you are seen, heard, and valued. A community needs you. An industry, office, non-profit, art class, meet-up, choir, house of worship, and village lack your skillset, song, and resolve. Your kindness, empathy, compassion, and grace are appreciated. You may not have found the right circles of support yet, but they are near. Keep pursuing those who bring out the best in you. Break free from negativity and toxicity. Find people who serve others and bring laughter. Smile. Listen. Care. Make others feel better when they are with you. Let them see greatness in the world and in themselves through your eyes. Let your goodness linger, even in hard conversations. Appreciate opportunity and accomplishment. Give thanks freely for each piece and person.

Let go of persistent distain. Listen for first responders. They are the valiant ones who protect, serve, and defend. They are also plain-clothed helpers arriving at your door in yoga pants or jerseys and shorts with a casserole of baked ziti in hand. There are others who are merely first to click emojis affirming or admonishing on social media when crises unfold. A fulfilling whole community is one where people readily attend and offer aid.

Look for gentleness and healing in meaningful actions and proactive change.

Love is the best, and often hardest reply. Where there is love, you are welcome.

5. Be light. Be bold. Be brave.

This is my mantra as I write this book. *Beautifully Broken* has been a part of my work and speaking for years, always with the intent of gathering all the notes and anecdotes into one source, but I waited. Interruptions prevailed. To live fully and wholly is to acknowledge interruptions.

Whole does not mean perfection. An astoundingly whole life is one filled with imperfections, authenticity, laughter, mess, beauty, hurt, passion, growth, and rest.

And more. There is always delicious, radical, wondrous more, if only we allow it.

6. Embrace "Yet I."

"Yet I" is a phrase of power or penalty. The difference rests in your view and choices. We can lead lives growing in grit, grace, hope, and love or focus on a façade of blame. It is a façade because we use blame as an excuse for poor choices and destructive responses. When faced with adversity and an ill-advised reply, we may rely on the explanation little children often use, "But they …" Accountability starts with owning our actions. We can do so wisely and powerfully by adopting a "Yet I" posture.

Trouble arises. It is not an *if* or *when* scenario. It does. Even if the waters rise or the well runs dry, even if they, she or he, behaves badly, you can choose the path of grit, grace, hope, and love. Those responses strengthen your stance. They further your mission. They empower you to overcome the seemingly impossible. They are concurrent short-term, interim, and long-range solutions.

Your "Yet I" of triumph are actions and attitudes in grit, grace, hope, and love.

- Inequality, social injustice, and darkness arise, yet I press on with love and light.
- Office stress, gossip, and whining are rampant, yet I choose to stay positive, focus on the good, and find solutions.
- I am tired and lost, yet I persist in sculpting new dreams.
- I am afraid, yet I will go.
- They plea for a "yes," yet I say, "no."
- A once sacred ground feels far from secure, yet I...
- Thirty-eight, three kids, cancer diagnosis, yet I...
- A relationship is not all I hoped for, yet I...

Let your rallying cry be, "Yet I."

For your whole life, know you are not alone, you are called to carry, and you are welcome.

Be bold and be brave.

Holding these precepts will unveil the components of your wonderful, overcoming and conquering "Yet I."

CHAPTER FOUR

BEAUTIFULLY BROKEN

Whenever I decide to do something with grit, grace, hope, and love, I usually make the right choice. If one of these components is absent while I conquer a case for a client, gather with friends and family, or co-parent our kids, I stumble, falter, and may fall. Worst still, I might bring others careening down with me.

The misstep may not be noticeable to those outside, but acting without grit, grace, hope, and love can lead to weighty scars of insecurity, hesitation, and fear. These are not traits we want leading us to courtrooms, boardrooms, and kitchen tables. Yet some of us are unknowingly bogged down by a barrage of self-doubt, worry, reluctance, and impatience, and we let these negatives drive our lives. Even tough seeming souls may appear to win battles, but with each crusade, they add to a vessel of pain, often widening wounds instead of mending and breaking free.

Years ago, my husband sent me flowers with a note saying, "I will love you your whole life." *Your whole life* - what a powerful descriptor of time, of me, of us. How do we find wholeness amid what is shattered? Every one of us in some small, marginal or vast ventricular way understands brokenness. To lead a *whole life*, we must see and accept *we are all beautifully broken.*

Before I was born, my mom and dad bought a blue and yellow, hand-painted, ceramic coffee pot as a wedding gift for another couple. It became ours when someone accidentally broke it and Mom carefully glued the pieces back together. As we moved to different houses, added breaks necessitated extra mending. Irrevocably cracked and some parts glistening with dried glue seeping from a tiny cut where a piece once fit, I don't know if other people entered our home and saw the beauty. Mom did. Handle and spout were dinged by all four of her children at one time or another over a twenty-year period. She centered this cracked pitcher in the living room. No hiding in a cupboard or corner. An ostensibly inconsequential vessel was crowned priceless amid brokenness.

Jagged, worn-out, and shattered is where light ignites. The world can be a breaking place and for every fracture there are a multitude of reparative beams.

When I was five, my favorite playground nestled against the beach. It offered the usual fare of monkey bars, swings, and slides, except for one odd outlier - an old train car, likely the locomotive cab. Windows broken out, rusted, and useless for going anywhere, it no longer roared on the rails. Children, however, found energy, imagination, and light (and hopefully no tetanus) climbing aboard. This ragged, broken engine carried a kingdom of beauty and hope.

Light breaks free through broken spaces. A darkened, self-imposed prison fills with hope when sunlight streams through a crack in the wall. You are wondrous. All of you, even the parts that keep messing up, the flaws and fragilities, each fragment is part of a miraculous mosaic. Layers of doubt, clouded by the grime and dirt of anger, sadness, and insecurity, may blind views of a masterful work of art. But know it is there. Ready for restoration. Every one of us experiences wrecks and ruptures, whether immediately onset or slowly corrosive, and it is here where light does its best work. The light comes in, ruminates, restores, and then illuminates all we encounter.

We fall, bounce back, amend, and amen.

Welcome the dream.

As children, we wildly, wonderfully, and freely dream. School years often begin with lists of questions, including one asking: When I grow I up I want to be _____?

We fill in the blank. We draw pictures. Somewhere, someone pushes it forward or sadly and abruptly crushes the hope for what may become. We grow up and grow out of lying down, looking at the sky, discovering cloud formations, and dreaming of our whole life ahead. With growth and knowledge, innocence sheds and we release some dreams perceiving they are childish and out of reach. Adult demands further set dreams aside. We grow old. We age long before we wrinkle and gray because our dreams lay dormant.

Not all lose their dreams; they merely lose their way. Others evolve. A once quiet hope is funded by strangers through crowd sourcing. The dream of riding the range as a cowboy moves to wrangling code in science and technology. A surfer stays close to the ocean, paddling her board on weekends and vacations, while during the week she rides innovative waves in advertising. A single mom writes during any spare moment, never letting go of her hope of one day penning a best seller.

Persistent dreamers cling to the confidence of *one day*. Though their pursuits may be lonely and laborious, they dauntlessly plow ahead. They persist despite rejection, boos, and labels. Paul McCartney doesn't just sing hits from forty years ago, he writes new songs and performs with young artists. He learns, creates, nurtures, and pursues. Younger generations may not know of his honorary knighthood and legendary career. McCartney is a rocker who wrote an opera, but they may not readily invite him to a party or might confuse him with an old relative of a relevant young star. So, what?

He listens to the song of his soul.

He sings the song of his soul.

He lives, and he is beautifully alive.

Nampeyo painted highly sought-after designs of her people in a unique genre, Hopi Revival pottery. Harriet Powers sewed stories on quilts later displayed in the National Museum of American History. Jackson Pollack painted revolutionary abstracts in drips and drops.

Through seams and brushes, with aching hands and bold offerings, they shared the songs of their souls.

Stephen King, Madeline L'Engle, and J. K. Rowling faced multiple rejections for their novels before their works became box office hits.

They wrote the songs of their souls.

They did not surrender their dreams.

There is a sacredness in holding each other's dreams. We live and breathe words. Dreams make them come alive.

When have you ever stopped dreaming? What pain or distraction quelled your passion?

Are you conscious, but asleep? For sleeping through life helps guard us from pain, but it also prevents us from soul-filling love and living a whole life.

It is time to come alive. Awaken your dreams.

It is time to sing the song of your soul.

It is time to help others sing.

Our chorus is the richness of a whole life.

Your dreams are the beautiful part of the child inside. They are the *you* of your youth, even if discovered at age forty or eighty. Dream on. Work hard in the realities of this world while dwelling in the dream. Enjoy the pursuit, for it is where you come alive.

Someone will be unkind to your dream. You paint, sing, write, build or simply mention an idea and dissenters pounce. You may be the first one to dismiss what you can become. Stop the self-destruction. A parent, sibling, teacher, or former friend may have said the one thing you hold onto that gives excuse for never fully becoming. Let go. Quit giving others the power to write your story.

Retain the dreams of childhood, not the ones of princes and astronauts riding dragons, but ones of colossal hope and wild joy. Mercies and majesties are not swayed by the burdens of bedtime and chores. Live in the freeing abandon of grit, grace, hope, and love.

The best stories of life are the ones of lost and found, of despair and renewal, of falling down and bouncing back with grit, grace, hope, and love.

Give yourself periodic pulse checks. Not on your heart rate, but on your hope rate. How are you feeling about what lies ahead? Is it the outcome you fear? Or the steps needed to get there? Perhaps both?

With trusted soul sisters and brothers, the one or two who bring out the best in you, ask:

Is this the life I am supposed to be living?

Grit, grace, hope, and love are not bound by zip codes, monetary status, politics, or any caste divide. Begin by being still each morning. Awake to mindfulness, prayer, and meditation. Our prayers are often monologuing through lists of concerns instead of purposeful reading, reactive listening, and waiting for insight and discernment. Be still, so you can become.

Give yourself grace. Set aside ten minutes to receive the goodness of gratitude and let your family know of your purposeful work. If your kids never see you read transformational books, if they never hear you meaningfully encourage yourself and others, if they do not know your hopes, prayers, and beliefs, how do you expect them to seek gifts of love? We watch a lot coming and going, posting and liking, but need to view more of living, thriving, and coming alive.

Tell yourself the words you need to hear. Speak what was never spoken. Offer the authentic assurance you needed but lacked while growing up. Tell your spouse, your kids, your friends, and your community words to beautifully become. Be in the business of building whole lives.

We are a concatenation of beings, bound by the soul-thriving beauty in carrying each other. Blessing you, blesses me. Clothing you, clothes me. Loving you, loves me. I may not see it now. A reply may confuse and confound me, but it should not halt me in the call to love.

Obstacles grow and hope wanes. Will you whine and wring the towel of "ain't it awful?" Or will you rise?

They say it's never going to happen? So, what?

Arise and come alive.

Rejected twenty, forty, sixty times? Maybe the sixty-first is the call you were waiting for. Pick up. Go. You are beautiful at sixty "no's." The "yes" does not define you, it propels you.

Be a dreamer who ignites and inspires.

Make Gentle.

There is a powerful, magnetic consequence of inspiration. It is too often untouched because of doubt and fear. Sometimes years pass before we recognize the significance of inspiration. But then there are seasons when nighttime's mourning awakens to a new day's joy. A fussy baby we are rocking and pleading to stop crying at 1:00 am is an irresistible miracle at 6:00 am. Same baby, but a different perspective. When joy takes hold, people do the unexpected. Impossible and unpredicted outcomes emerge. Grit, grace, hope, and love unfold. We discover good within and find it was present all along. We simply missed it, like glimmers of light in darkness.

On April 4, 1968, the evening of the assassination of Dr. Martin Luther King, Jr., Bobby Kennedy arrived in Indianapolis for a campaign speech and learned of Dr. King's death. Local police advised Senator Kennedy not to make his speech because he was appearing in a perceived dangerous part of the city. Undaunted, the senator arrived finding a crowd filled with campaign excitement, unaware of the tragic death. He climbed onto the back of a flatbed truck and told of how Dr. King died in the pursuit of justice for all.

Kennedy assured he understood the pain and anger felt when an assassin takes the life of one you love, and he spoke of the imperative need in our nation for unity, love, wisdom, and compassion toward one another.

Kennedy closed his remarks with a prayer and benediction, saying, in part,

"Let us dedicate ourselves to what the Greeks wrote so many years ago: to tame the savageness of man and make gentle the life of this world."

Indianapolis, a town fraught with racial tension, experienced no riots that night. Senator Kennedy didn't choose this calm. The people of Indianapolis did. He, and many others, inspired peace and light in darkest hours. Martin Luther King, Jr. encouraged all to lead lives of love. Weeping, wisdom, and the work of love prevailed.

To tame the savageness and make gentle the life, we must start from within. It begins with working on the gaps and holes preventing our wholeness. We must determine where we are and the direction we want our lives to take. Living a life of love means doing the hard work of wholeness. It includes letting someone go, but doing so with grace and integrity. It means crossing a room to greet someone you may not want to stand beside for an entire evening. It means taking a stand for what is right. It means being there for others even when the only present solution is simply to take a seat at their table. It means taking a breath before blasting out our immediate reaction. We come to adulthood with wounds. Excessive eating, anger, alcohol, sex, pain killers, distractions, and wanton spending are flimsy patches. We shove globs of gunk into holes, only to mask but never mend. Whole living commences as we fill holes with grit, grace, hope, and love. Grieve and cleave. Mourn what should have been said and done. Lament. Get angry. Acknowledge loneliness and pain. And then go on in love. Cut off the lies of self-hate. Forgive.

Oh forgiveness, the holy ground for healing! Lack of forgiveness happens when you and I stand in the quick sand of memories. We hurt not just because of what was said today, but for what it conjures from twenty years ago. Grace pulls us out of the pit. Grace gives us strength to forgive, bringing us to the place where we stop sipping the poison and move from false-self to full life. Grace helps us grab unwavering truths:

Beautiful, imperfect, loved, tired, stinky, wonderful, ornery, worthy, capable, and enough.

This is you. This is me. This is us.

To tame and make gentle, breathe in, count to ten and hold it. Exhale with assuring words to yourself on what's happening and how you are feeling before wielding anger and angst on social media or at anyone in your radius. The difference between healing or hurting, success or defeat, may be found in those ten seconds.

The waiting is the hardest part. In my early twenties, I'd roll my eyes after hearing deep breathing techniques recommended to anyone other than women in labor. Back then, immediately getting to task made me feel better. Age brought wisdom and necessity for sacred spaces. Places where I can breathe, read, and restore.

Routinely engaging in mindful, quiet moments spiritually recharges and rests your soul. Negative thoughts may arise at any time. The key is what to do with them. Gauge yourself. Is your initial reaction to yell or be still? Will you forgive so you may abundantly live?

What will you abandon for abundance?

Forgiveness is a radical renovation of your soul. It is not about the other person, forgiveness is for you. Hate destroys the vessel that carries it; whereas forgiveness is a new creation.

Choose to live in love.

Are you plugging along or powerfully pursuing?

Do you pause for your present achievements or are you so focused on the next goal you lose sight of enjoying or living in the moment?

There is a rich, precious, paramount gift in recognizing daily choices.

Overcome or come undone.

Integrity or dishonesty.

Patience or irritation.

Kindness or cruelty.

Love or hate.

In the face of injustice, corruption, despair, and silence we choose our reply. When social media is filled with friends' posts of exotic Spring Break travel and you are vacationing in Bora Bora, it is easier to respond well. But if at home where everyone has the stomach flu radiating from every orifice, not so much.

Careless leadership results in falling for - or conceding to - the excuse, "I had no choice." It's a lie we tell ourselves to defend bad decisions.

Living in love is living in the hard place of delayed gratification. A super hero's strength does not activate from her home planet or cape. Her power initiates when she chooses to save or sit still. What makes super men and wonder women? Determining the most loving thing to do and acting on it.

Managers share this power. One of the hardest components of managing people is deciding when to throw a life preserver or offer a ship to another shore. In our desire to avoid negativity and confrontation, we keep people in roles when the most loving thing to do is let go. Get the employee into a new role as quickly as possible that best fits their skillset whether in the present company or elsewhere.

Here rests the bulldogged hard work of the efficacious, brave, and mighty. Choosing to live in love is continually assessing what is best for the company and employees; it is choosing what is best for a friendship or family and each of its members. *Knowing what's best* is not an exact science. My dad taught us that love includes the courage to cut, coach, and confront. Without love, these acts are destructive. With love, they fix, train, and foster gratitude. Love empowers tough decisions leading to better outcomes.

I remember when a friend awaited a prison sentence. We stood with him. He had a family, a home, a dog, a company and he lost everything awaiting his sentence. As an Assistant District Attorney, I recommended prison sentences and sought jury convictions. Determining the right recommended outcome for any crime is a solemn task.

Our friend faced an appropriate consequence. We talked a lot before he reported to prison. He said, "My whole life I was ahead of everything. Ahead in school, ahead in the market. Now I'm behind. What's ahead is prison. I'm waiting, and I'm scared of all the unknown."

There is power in waiting. Power in uncertainty. Power offering release, no matter where or how long the sentence. Power emerges with diligent practice. You see strength surface in the presence of fear.

Stress and pain are relative. Each life is filled with mess and joy, much of which we create. At one time or another, we have all lived our own country ballad. I wonder if a group or solo star would sing my current refrain:

"Welcome to Dysfunction Junction.
Our house sits in the square."

Uncomfortable, hard, aggravating, confusing circumstances are places where light does its best work, if we let it in. Living a whole life with grit, grace, hope, and love means we welcome the light. We acknowledge darkness. We do not vanquish emanating good. We relish, renew, and release. Light does not stand still; it imparts. Anger, insecurity, doubt, boredom, jealousy, and worry squash and distort light's resplendent glow. We do this to ourselves and each other. We choose what we illuminate.

To tame and make gentle.

To become what we are called to be.

To live a whole life.

We need grit, grace, hope, and love.

Listen.

On our last day of vacation, finishing off dessert for breakfast, our youngest, Gabrielle Joy, pronounced:

"I'm sorry, birthday cake ice cream is the best."

I replied, "Sweetie, you do not have to begin your opinion with an apology."

She said, "I was apologizing to strawberry."

I missed the message.

We spend an exhaustive amount of time focused on what we say instead of what we hear. Listening is the art of exceptional trial lawyers, CEOs, parents, and friends. Zeroing in on your message without hearing the other side leads to stalemates and lopsided verdicts. Anticipating answers is helpful when preparing for a discussion but doing so in the midst causes harm.

Relationships start with listening. Contracts commence with listening for they require offer, acceptance, and consideration. Active listening requires engaging all the senses to hear the message conveyed. Why then do smart spouses, executives, siblings, parents, and friends neglect this apparent skill? We know the right thing to do, but our minds can only receive a finite amount of information. We often miss what is right in front of us. Becoming aware of what we missed causes awe and regret.

"Oh, I never noticed."

No big deal if it's a flower. Big problem if it's a railroad crossing, and the train is barreling down the tracks.

Sensory overload diminishes our ability to see. Multi-tasking is a drain on the heart and head. Miracles and masterpieces abound far beyond anything on our to-do lists. If we are not careful, an infiltrating influx leads to missing magic. We need to rewire our belief that to be mighty we must multi-task.

Whenever possible listen to wise counsel, including your own. Trust your gut.

A sight to behold, not put in your mouth.

A few years ago, my husband and I were filled with uncertainty. At the time, we had a sick child, work stress from wondering how things might shake out for my company in the economy, a board seat in a struggling organization, and transition to a new school. One day I was pondering about this while in carpool. For those who have not experienced carpool, it is place where drivers are supposed to be at the immediate ready. It is akin to people arriving at court. It is a hurry-up and wait process.

Phones off, no cars idling. Hands on the wheel, looking ahead as a traffic cop motions you in for pick-up. Lingering is frowned upon. Hurry-up, pile them in. Get moving. Unless you arrive early in the carpool lane. The first few in line can read, reply to texts and emails, return calls or, in my case on this particular day, clean the car. While I might feel pride because my car is not a minivan, there is no such acceptable boasting for this family SUV looks like the bottom of my purse. (I think I just simultaneously put down my purse and organizational skills.) Books, art supplies, and water bottles were ample for the distracted and hungry, along with receipts, clothes, remnants of parties and meals consumed as we rushed sweaty kids to and from fields of play.

Climbing over rows of seats with deft and dexterity, I collected trash, wiped down the dash board and car seats and basked in immediate gratification. Until I realized I'd lost my keys while in my cleaning frenzy. Frantically opening every door, I searched. It was hot, I was sweating, worried the carpool procession would begin and I'd have to wave everyone by with "Sorry, lost my keys. Can you believe it? Yes, I know. Crazy, right? So sorry."

The keys finally emerged and as I returned to the driver's seat, a friend knocked on the window. A huge smile covered his face. I didn't know if he'd observed my clean car lost key adventure.

When I opened the window to greet him, he immediately gave me a fist bump. I bumped back not realizing he had something in his hand. He dropped the item into mine. With a dusty black interior and trash no long reflecting sunlight, it was kind of dark in my car. I opened my hand under his and saw my friend offered a piece of chocolate. How thoughtful. I love dark chocolate. I popped it into my mouth.

Only it wasn't chocolate.

As I tossed it into my mouth, my friend cried, "No, no!"

Too late.

I carefully took it out of my gaping mouth and grabbed hand sanitizer to clean this non-edible item before returning it. I didn't know what it was, and it did not taste good.

My friend smiled and shared, "Twelve years ago I was going through a hard time and somebody gave me this acorn to remind me of all that is possible."

My friend was tender as he released his treasure. He said, "It's hard to let it go, but I think you need this today."

His beautiful acorn rested in my palm. Its design is lovely, unique, and easily missed. It is filled with holes. Through those holes I saw a symbol of hope.

What do you hold to remind you of all that is possible?

Our oldest, Jack, loves army men and action figures. His set ups are intricate, marvelous masterpieces. I'm a mom. I have a keen eye for this sort of thing. The figures often fill a large table outside on our deck. I don't take them down until he is ready. The natural background of the great outdoors helps make the tiny statues come alive. Jack and his siblings create stop action movies. These plastic figures engender imagination, play, and comfort while boosting mathematic and spatial reasoning. Okay, that last part is a pious add on, when all I need to say is they make my kids happy.

One day, Jack wondered if he was too old to play with army men and action figures. I told him I want him to always keep some in his pocket or at his desk. When he's twenty, forty or seventy-five, he can pull them out, hold them, and feel hope.

It is important to hold on to hope.

It is good to grasp grace.

What do you hold in your hand?

What do you recall to remind you of all that is possible?

What sets your focus back on love?

Awake and arise to your dreams.

Find these reminders. Be these reminders for others.

We are called to love. It is a maxim and a mandate. It is the work of warriors. There is no segment of life inaccessible to a loving act. Fear, anger, insecurity, and doubt muck with the ebb of love. Stillness and rest revive the flow.

Beautifully becoming.

Is it our power or ignorance that scares us most?

Is it easier to squelch our beautiful, unique, wonderfully possible selves than vulnerably stand in love's truths?

Am I afraid of authenticity or what I believe others will see?

Or, do I fear they'll find the façade? The perfectly adorned room captured on social media is a narrow glimpse. Edited edges hide the piles of laundry, chipped paint, and the random piece of gum stuck to the floor.

You don't have to share it all to be it all.

A common, unspoken fear is the fear of getting found out. *Imposter Syndrome* is a pervasive feeling of inadequacy despite evidence to the contrary. Although prevalent for centuries, people often think they are alone in this overwhelming doubt. Most of us have felt the fraud lie at some point in a job, dating, or parenting. It is a conquerable loneliness. The solution rests in acknowledging the fear, desiring change, and seeing your valuable worth as you are right now. It is the gift of accepting *you are becoming.*

I remind young lawyers when they are feeling overwhelmed and thinking every attorney and client knows more than they do to remember they are expertly trained at research. They are not expected to immediately have the answer; they are hired to *carefully find* the right one.

Social media elevates comparison. We view highlights as aggregates of daily life forgetting that filters can dull reality. We heighten a risk-adverse mindset because it appears everyone is hashtagging a life of sustained awe and wonder.

We spend so much time perfecting what we put out, we miss seeing what is inside. We deny ourselves the gift of processing problems with wise, trusted problem-solvers. Instead, we leap into comparing our perceived lack with someone else's alleged all. Incorporating grit, grace, hope, and love into our steps and sights helps push out the false narrative.

A little self-doubt can help us work harder and improve. Too much leads to debilitating, unseen anxiety. Authentically infused grit, grace, hope, and love empower us to show ourselves as we are. Instead of being led by fear, make art out of the arduous. See the good in yourself and others and avoid being blinded by defeating thoughts.

We crave online stimulation to distract the pain of aloneness. Scrolling through feeds amplifies our isolation. We sit in crowds and look down at our devices. We are lonely en masse, pushed into absolutes of political positions, gender parity, race, and caste. Find connections of hope and joy. Build compassionate communities.

Look up. Don't let one hurtful moment or comment pierce your identity, when those fragments do not define your whole.

You are worthy and loved – where you are, as you are.

You are enough.

You are beautifully becoming.

CHAPTER FIVE

OUR DWELLING PLACE

Leonardo Da Vinci is credited with conveying, "Small rooms or dwellings discipline the mind; large ones weaken it." If this is true, my pantry is a dwelling of intellectual prowess. Its corners are respite for popcorn kernels and dog food gone astray from intended containers. Center shelves hold nice looking, wine-filled racks. I try to quickly open favorites for friends as this tiny closet offers no temperature control. We live in an old ranch-style house. The pantry was once a small linen closet. I'm sure if fully cleaned it would reveal remnants of original shelf paper or at least a hint of the glue.

Our pantry is just off the kitchen and likely should have remained a linen closet given the minimal closet space offered by early 1950s architects. With four kids, I wanted somewhere to toss economy-size, volume buys. A step stool, stack of baskets, and a collection of large wooden bowls cover most of the floor. It gives room to store our bounty and is the doorway to dry good provisions. It is a room of ready weakness and strength depending largely on supply and demand. When the door is open, you don't step inside, you peer in, stretch, and grab what is desired, or at least what will placate before yelling, "Does anybody know where the cookies are?" Followed by, without awaiting reply, "Who ate all the cookies?"

When I was little, we didn't have a pantry. Things went in a kitchen cabinet or on top of the fridge.

In an interview with a famous talk show host I heard two of my favorite singers discuss how they keep their love alive with small children in the house. With marriage, work, and kids, the prolific interviewer wondered how they maintain light in their eyes. They looked at each other, smiled, and shared how they care for each other. They are friends and partners. They work on their relationship and know it is a blessing to guard and nurture. To do so, they make time for quick, romantic getaway moments in the house. One favorite escape is the pantry.

I hoped the interviewer would ask my follow-up question, *"How big is your pantry?"*

You can't walk into mine without stepping on something one may or may not be able to define. Dried seaweed has a similar crunch to gluten-free, quinoa-based noodles. Oh shoot, and now there is a question of whether quinoa has too many chemicals, or maybe we should eliminate certain seeds along with the metallic organic canned tomatoes which may contain impurities. Good gravy, just bring on the cheese-flavored, not-found-in-nature orange crunchy snacks! One look into this full pantry and you could decide to throw in the towel and head out to dinner. There is a space for each item, but they end up tossed aside in the frantic search for cookies.

The interview sticks with me and I mention it to my husband, Chris. We call him "Sully." When I was little, there was a funny, kind *Sesame Street*® character called, "Sully." Perhaps my love for him and the name began there. We agree there is more room in an airplane bathroom than our pantry. And one is sans any anti-bacterial soap or a lock.

Still, it stays on my mind. They keep their love alive with fun getaways in the pantry.

Some argue birthdays are significant when they end in a zero or five. Every birthday is noteworthy and cause for commemoration, for if you are alive, there is significant, purposeful, unique work left to do. Each deserves celebration, and fortunately on one of mine, friends gave us the joy of meeting this couple who find romance in their pantry. Their love was evident. Their grace and gratitude filled the space between us. Arrogance and distance could have sprung, but they seemed purposeful in knowing what is important, sacred, and worthy. They still sing. He acts. Time does not dull their compassion, wit, and laugh lines. They both seem frozen in beauty because of an inward and outward lack of wrinkles joined with thankfulness and love.

They live large lives and dwell in small sanctuaries. I'm sure their home is a rambling ranch with horse-filled acres and immense, warm rooms. Tight jeans and cowboy hats. They look great in both, surely due to averting any sugary, carb-filled loot hidden in the pantry.

Living whole lives and striving for all they can become, they dwell in small sacred spaces. Doing so, they protect the power of intangible treasures found in relationships. They abide in abundant grit, grace, hope, and love.

Dwell here.

Where we dwell matters. Where we linger shapes our thoughts and choices. Struggle, unrest, bad things, unexpected pain, annoying co-workers, pessimistic bosses, and unpleasant Thanksgiving dinner conversations will come. Sometimes it all happens at the same table. You dwell in a chaotic ping pong of frustration. At other points, it is one big problem, muting all else. A medical issue arises and everything else is set aside. Then come waves from the daily grind, crashing one onto the next.

Instead of dwelling on "what if something goes wrong," we need to approach life with joyful expectation. Not with false-hope or poorly prepared plans. Not with cheer, as if one of Thomas Paine's sunshine patriots, offering affirming words only when we feel good. It is a decision to work in sustaining grit, grace, hope, and love no matter the circumstance.

Mindfully prepare each day with a "what if" outlook of optimism. Carry an attitude of innovation. Don't let it rest solely with entrepreneurs and engineering graduates. You are the innovator of your life. Secure the right source for restoration.

Replace worry with a presumption of wonder. To do this, you must practice. Thoughtfully choose where you dwell each day. Consider the noise you let in and what you drown out. Become aware of when you are weary. Your heart is where you spend most of your time and money. (As I write, this might mean my family currently dwells in Mexican and Thai food.)

You are not permanently stuck in a mire mindset. It is not too late. You are not defined by a present circumstance.

Change begins with answering two questions.

I ask executives two questions before consulting commences. These questions apply to each of us in work and life. I've utilized these queries in working with schools to improve special education services. I've asked them of myself when going through a hard time. They are a start, and then need repeating throughout the journey.

1. Is there a sickness?
2. Do you want to get well?

Is there a sickness? In other words, is there a problem, a weakness, an area needing improvement?

In a corporate setting, employees may want to get well, but a poor performing supervisor may not recognize there is a problem. Or there is the entrepreneur who foolishly forgets to focus on and sell the why - the problem she is solving - and instead stays lost in the what.

One person may take up so much time and space they cannot see their lack of listening and empathy is destroying a relationship.

Or a person who seems larger than life may have open wounds no one can see, those of a lonely, abusive childhood, and the hidden hurt prevents him from ever wanting to root himself in deep love.

On a ball field, it's bleacher parents moving to the sidelines screaming obscenities. Rules of play state: "Do not shout instructions; suffer in silence; and refrain from obscenities," but some parents do not think the rules apply to all. They do not see their behavior as a problem. The referee can and will stop the match if the crowd becomes discourteous. Love requires us to act in the best interest of others, including identifying strengths and weaknesses, offering ways to improve and implementing agreed upon consequences.

Do you want to get well? Do you want things to change and improve? Is it more comfortable to stay in the present circumstance than do the right thing? A friend explains it like this: "My first marriage headed to divorce the moment I walked down the aisle. I knew we weren't supposed to be together, but it seemed like the next thing to do after dating through college. I guessed it seemed easier than breaking up and being alone."

I may loathe my job, but the prospect of searching and starting over is daunting. Although I complain, I am immobile, unwilling to find relief. My stress becomes my deprivation and strangulation instead of serving as a catalyst for getting well.

A teenager may repeatedly forget her homework and sports gear, but if mom and dad readily bring it to school in response to every pleading text, there is no impetus to get well.

Change is . . .

Hard. Necessary. Frustrating. Scary. Good. Not always growth or a better way forward. Natural. Life.

Change is an invitation to progress. While we might face change kicking and screaming, it comes whether we want it or not. You can fight change or dance with it. The moves, mood, and melody lie within.

Without meditative patience and a strong, positive community influence, you may wall yourself up in layered wounds mortared with self-righteous convictions, passive-aggressive jabs, and poisoning silence. It's astounding how people can live off hate and hurt without acknowledging the corrosive decay. Transformation treads on a tightrope. We sway and may wallow in misery or swim in joy. We fare far better with trusted relationships on our journey. Healthy tribes offer the support and push to go on with grit, grace, hope, and love.

You are in control of your life. You take the lead. Your co-workers, family, friends, and strangers are impacted by your actions and inactions. Be a friend, not an enemy, to your soul. Celebrate what it means to live a whole life. Joy is the way.

Today, ask yourself these questions:

1. Is there a stress, illness, or burden needing relief?
2. Do I want to get well?

Let us proceed. Let us strengthen, heal, and renew our whole lives. We can do this. No matter your age, you can never exhaust growing in grit, grace, hope, and love.

Believe in all you are and will become. Find healthy places to put the pain. Stop going to dry wells to replenish a thirsty soul.

Dwell in sacred spaces of encouragement, wonder, restoration, reflection, and joy.

Perhaps including the pantry.

Call and claim
your hallelujahs.
Have the courage to be.
You are not the sum
of all they see.

CHAPTER SIX

GRIT

You are lionhearted.

Go. Press on in your authenticity.
Rise, roam, and roar.

It may be grander, harder,
and muddier than you imagined.

Continue in your courage.
Help others find their roar.

Press On.

The path I run is a road to history. It is my story. My pains, my joys. Milestones reached and sometimes conquered while wandering in the wilderness. My rest. My sprint. My crawl. My stride. My victory.

This is my life and it is your life too. Every story is unique because it is yours to tell. Your race of life is yours to finish. There are no time trials or ribbons for win, place, or show. It is the pace you set for yourself as needed and desired. It is the conquering of little things to move toward a greater goal. Living a whole, fulfilling, abundant life is running to your dreams, sharing the road, asking for assistance and nourishment along the way, and stopping to carry and encourage others. It means knowing when to look back and when to move on. It requires preparation, times of teamwork, and periods of isolation. New routes and relationships will come. Rest and stamina are required. To finish, you will fall, fail, and rise.

Embrace the whole race. Keep sight of your vision and mission. Press on with faith and assurance. This is the challenge and reward.

A run, a playlist, and the pursuit.

My weight is at an all-time low. This is a claim I have not uttered, ever. Recently, I decided to run to get in shape, to tone and tighten. I do so to show our kids that health is a matter of getting out and doing. Go. No qualifiers needed. Just, go. Run.

While a personal in-home trainer is ideal, putting on shoes and getting out the door has fewer financial barriers. The cost is time, pain, and persistence. My current run is arduous. Not so for many, but for me. I am getting fitter and try to run five miles most mornings. "Try" is the optimal word. The first mile is dull. I do not like to run. Better said, I loathe it! At times I finish mile one when it's cold and rainy and consider calling my husband for a ride home after a quick swing into Starbucks®. Immediate gratification, instead of delayed. Our friends Felicia, Rebecca, Julie, and Ann encouraged me and taught me it is good to walk a bit when I need to and to sprint as often as I can. I'm training and getting better. Each morning I press on.

The first two and half miles are the hardest. The journey home is easier. I return on the same path I began, but my focus changes because

I am heading home. With love in sight, I press on.

My path is a road to history, not just because of my own tales to share. My half way mark is the Atlanta History Center. Parts of Atlanta's history are the painful wounds of racism. We continue to hurt and heal. I reach the Center and keep going to strengthen my core. Overcoming what is behind, I press on.

On the journey, I notice what people discard. A pair of high heels, mail, fast food wrappers, empty soda cans and beer bottles, a car bumper, a heavy piece of metal fencing, a condom wrapper. I wonder if any are tossed due to an urgent desire at forty miles per hour. Perhaps, they too, press on.

In living a whole life, we press on. In every journey we take, we discard, cling to, and carry. But we also set aside. These are things we are not yet ready to throw away, so we keep them out of sight because we are unsure if we will need them later.

Runners take their mark and leave their mark. On this particular path, my mark is identified on the sidewalk. It is our oldest son's initials and mine carved on the pavement. We marked a day of wet concrete and mischief ten years ago. When I catch this spot, it carries me on.

So does my playlist.

Music lifts and invigorates. It stirs our creative souls and fires focus. The tempo combined with memories impact mood and motivation. What songs immediately amp you up to perform when little is left in you? They are the melodies prompting us to dance in the kitchen or finish the race.

Sometimes I walk, sometimes I run. Active, brave, loving, frustrated, stumbling on crumbling concrete, hopeful. Occasionally stopping to chat with people on the way or offering a smile as another runner passes. Listening for what might awaken ideas, solutions, and peace. This is my morning ritual. I press on.

If I miss a day or two and indulge in a slice of cake or two, I give myself grace and try to avoid the scale. Running is easier when I have company. The miles go faster when a friend and I walk and run together. Pushing each other beyond a pounding march to a joyful pace, we solve a myriad of problems and laugh. We bid, "Goodbye," and are ready for what might await in the day ahead. We press on.

How do we persevere through life's complex races?

How do we conquer the hard, beautiful, treacherous, and good?

How do we consistently persist? What ignites us to press on?

What is an excellent indicator for success?

Grit.

The gift of grit.

Grit predicts success. More than IQ or innate talent, grit is an overwhelming determinant for ultimate attainment. Grit is robust, strength of character. It is tenacity, perseverance, and passion for the pursuit of long-term goals and is a stronger indicator of future earnings and happiness than an IQ score or a particular talent.

Angela Duckworth, Malcolm Gladwell, and my mom and dad have long contended this truth. (*See Grit, Outliers, and my kitchen table.*) "Grit" is not a ready part of our lexicon. Read an obituary and you are unlikely to find "He was gritty" as an attribute for a life well lived, but it is.

We ought to consider character traits we admire but are reluctant to convey. Perhaps this is because we are unsure how to define them.

I grew up in a household with a lot of love, but few things. Mom and Dad encouraged us to press on, fight for the underdog, love each other, look out for others, pray often, give passionately and generously, work hard, be present, and offer people a seat at the table. We lived out their examples, sometimes to their fear, frustration, and admiration.

One evening at the dinner table our family discussed the 1960s bus boycotts and the importance of standing up so others can sit. The next day I was riding the bus home from school and saw my chance to take a stand. It was a middle school bus in a small Florida town. Stickiness on any surface touched. Riding this bus was a jolting jaunt because the driver would not stay in any gear for long and it was a bus full of young, pre-cellphone-occupied teenagers. As my friend got off the bus at her stop, the driver made a derogatory comment. He used inappropriate language for anyone to describe someone else, let alone an adult describing a young teenage girl. Shock stunned me for a moment. I think the doors closing and his readiness to move into another gear forced me to get up. I purposefully walked up the aisle to the bus driver and demanded, "You need to stop the bus and let me off *now!*" He asked why and I explained, "I won't stay on this bus. You can't talk to us that way. I can't stop you from talking, but I can get off this bus." I gave him a set of fierce eyes only a teenage girl can deftly utilize. I didn't budge. He did. He stopped, opened the door, and I got off.

I arrived home later than expected.

Mom was worried. "Where were you?"

Relieved. "Oh, I'm so glad you are okay."

Then Mom held a furrowed brow as she asked for explanations. "Now tell me exactly what happened."

As I examine that day now, it was weird the driver didn't say anything and backed down to a kid. He did inform the principal who called my parents that night stating I violated school rules. This was a first and being first at something when you are third born is usually a proud moment. The hardest part was telling my mother the words he used. We didn't talk that way in our house. I was awed as I spit them out and she didn't look surprised. Mom understood.

Dad got home. He heard the story and smiled. He said I was gritty. Later, I realized it was Mom and Dad who were gritty in their parenting. I could not hear the phone conversation with the principal. I could only see my mom and dad's expressions as they listened. Kind, thoughtful, firm, and resolute. The next day we had a new bus driver.

You can garner grit.

Grit is stick-to-itiveness.

Grit is resilience, trust, an indomitable spirit despite setbacks, a character of consistent courage in peaks and valleys, and strength for the long haul, *and it is something you can learn.*

Getting gritty is possible at any age. No matter your present circumstance and position, you can grow in grit. Your burdens, gifts, and steadfast dreams form the backbone of grit.

Living a whole life means you choose each day to grow and empower others to become gritty. Your whole life, the completeness and wonder of you, is emboldened when you fortify others with goodness. Grit is part of the good.

College admissions teams and corporate recruiters can spend a great deal of time focused on lesser metrics. Good grades, high test scores, unique talents, and solid references are all fine attributes, but consider the exponential opportunities for prosperity if we invest in grit. Instead of looking merely at personality and potential, companies should also ingrain and grow grit. Talent may get the job, but character will build the career.

Arguably, targeting and hiring gritty people, and strengthening grittiness within a team or family, are somewhat illusive. Grit can be hard to quantify. It is defined, in part, by persistence and it takes persistence to spot it and ultimately grow it. We need to put employees and children in situations to help them grow in grit and provide the tools to do so through access, role-play, and mentorship.

Our models for education and achievement can push more people away from paths of poverty and prison if we incorporate growing in grit, grace, hope, and love into our development strategies. These are the lenses through which we should plan our actions. They are the foundations we should build upon. In doing so, we foster the military precept that is a battle cry of the gritty: improvise, adapt, and overcome.

A healthy dose of grit.

True grit does not grow in isolation. Nor does it overpower reason.

Too much grit prompts athletes to play while injured leading to debilitating, career-ending pain. Too much grit causes CEOs to stay so focused on the mission, they fail to pause, pivot, and adjust strategies. Grit should not get in the way of common sense. A downhill skier who sees the tree ahead and has time to avoid a crash, should change her path. An unwillingness to do anything other than stay the course can alienate all around you. Laser focus on long-term goals is good. Getting trapped in a dead end is not. Knowing when and how to let go is better.

Like salt, the right amount of grit is beneficial to our lives. Salt is purifying, cleansing, and preserving. It nourishes and adds flavor. Eating too much causes dehydration, soaring blood pressure, and puts strain on the heart, kidneys and brain. Too little, and its benefits are diluted. We need salt and grit as we grow into all we are called to be. Living a whole, abundant life means garnering the right amount of grit and coupling it with kindness, gratitude, compassion, intellect, and humility.

People with healthy grit do three things:

1. Believe.
2. Make room for the impossible.
3. Adapt.

I. Believe.

Belief is confident, dogged determination.

Authentic, whole, gritty people are risk-takers. They believe *outrageous thoughts* like:

- I trust myself, and I believe in my ability to tackle obstacles.
- I rely on faith and remember hard times I've already overcome.
- I am comfortable with "I don't know," and "let's try."
- I will break free from my self-made prisons.
- My wounds, flaws, and differences are the very things that can be redeemed and used for magnificent good.

An approaching tropical storm brought Atlantans stampeding to super markets for bottled water, batteries, and a colossal supply of cookies. Power outages call for board games and junk food provisions. When I arrived at the grocery store, there were few treats to find and no water. I'm a Florida girl and remember the days of filling bathtubs with water during hurricanes. I ran into a friend and we hugged and shared our kids' excitement for missing a day of school and a night spent huddled in the basement. As we said goodbye, a woman behind me snapped, "This is a time to shop, not socialize. Get moving!"

Pierced lips and disapproving eyes locked on me. On a different day, one when I felt less than or weary, her reaction may have rattled me and stuck. "Good gravy! Okay lady, let's dial it back!" is what I (maybe we) might want to demand. But this day, I didn't let this woman rob my joy. I saw her hurt. I reacted with a smile and love. I didn't let her choices change my beliefs.

I did text my friend while still in the store:

"Ooooooh, you're in trouble."

And texted again proposing new overhead music selections to stir singing in the rain:

"It's time for some Aretha anthems or dearly beloved Prince."

Sometimes we are the ones with road rage - whether behind a cart or the wheel.

To live a whole life requires a willingness to believe radical truths. They are radical and outrageous because they oppose a world of negativity and destruction. Gritty people know love is more powerful than hate. They move their knowing into doing. They respond with truth in love even when their initial emotion is anger. One person can impact the whole of what you believe, if you let them. Every day you can choose to use this power for good. Consider what you believe and what you impart.

People who garner authentic grit hold fast to the good, even when the hard becomes life.

Be gracious and giving. Hold audacious ambition and combine it with constant pursuit. Abide in strength and lead in love. From mistakes and falls, apologize, forgive, and rise. See the upside. Press on.

People who grow in grit are cautious of who whispers in their ear. They are optimistic in their view of "*What else could I become?*"

There is an old story my dad often told of two men born of an abusive, alcoholic father. One lived a life of despair. Brokenness continued with multiple divorces, lost jobs, addictions, destroyed relationships, and isolation. The other son pursued hope and grew in gratitude. He fulfilled dreams and saw his wife and children succeed. Each son had difficulties and great sadness. Neither were assured success, fortune, or health. They shared potential for joy, if chosen. One brother living in darkness, the other in light. Both knew hardships, but one believed and overcame. When each was asked, "How did your life unfold this way?" They each replied, "What else could I become?"

Belief strengthens with faith. When faith is tested, endurance has a chance to grow.

Believing in goodness, trusting outcomes, having faith in dark, desolate circumstances or on expressways when someone gives you the middle finger - these are the work of grit.

2. Make room for the impossible.

Noble tasks seem insurmountable at the onset. A wedge of light makes room for the impossible. Light does not remove challenges. It reminds us to dream and allows us to walk out goals we want to achieve. With grit, we walk in light.

After the collapse and destruction of 9-11, America rebuilt and restored. Newness arose amongst heartache. Broken pieces became monuments of hope. We grew from Ground Zero to memorials beaming light. Seeing what is erected in New York now, and remembering shattered lives and ash-filled streets, we recognize beauty unfolding in brokenness. America made room for the impossible. America let in light.

In the everyday cycle of work and life, we may fail to make room for light. Our labors, suffering, and sorrow ramrod optimism. Envy blinds and distorts our perspective. We pull up the covers, shut the doors, and have no room to let in the idea of achieving the seemingly impossible. Apprehension and anxiety obstruct. Fear is a snake impeding goals, setting limits on capabilities and strangling creativity.

You cannot outlive your utility. Your breath signifies there is time to figure out how to be. Much of it lies in finding stillness and peace. Accept there is a sense of peace capable of surpassing any problem. Decide to be a wedge of light to others, even while trudging through your own momentary darkness. A wedge of light is the powerful activation of joy.

Consider what makes you timid. We are created for strength, love, and self-discipline. So much of what shapes us is what we believe and accept as comparisons. Let a wedge of light bring truth to dispel doubt.

The awesome and astounding rest under a veil of the seemingly impossible. Grit removes the barrier. It tears the veil separating us from truth and wonder.

Gritty people make room for the impossible.

They, you and me, try and try and try.

We don't let labels stick. We carry on. We let light in.

We believe in the impossible before breakfast.

We recognize light may come from a small safe place where companionship, a smile or a hug are welcome.

This is the stuff of grit.

3. Adapt.

If you spend an afternoon fly fishing and catch nothing, you change the fly, move to a different spot on the river, or pack up and go home. You do not change the fish. People who strive for whole, abundant living follow the advice of St. Augustine to keep adding, keep walking, and keep advancing.

Children grow, economies shift, science, technology, and relationships evolve. If we adapt, we thrive.

When researcher and virologist Jonas Salk was asked to explain how he invented one of the first successful polio vaccines, it is said he replied, "I pictured myself as a virus or cancer cell and tried to sense what it was like to be."

Dr. Salk did not lose sight of his goal to eradicate polio. He adapted his thinking to conquer the disease.

Achieving your mission will require pivots in strategy. Resourceful, scrappy, positive - these are three monikers my parents said would help my siblings and me achieve in our chosen paths. These monikers have aided me in every aspect of my legal career, whether as a trial lawyer or consultant. Resourceful, scrappy, and positive are also the mindsets of a mom when she learns at 9:30 pm multiple ingredients are needed for preparing tomorrow's seventh grade science project, or so I'm told.

On my first day as an assistant district attorney, they had no office ready for me. I'd left a nice, well-respected downtown labor and employment law firm because I wanted more trial work. As labor lawyers representing companies, we tended to try our cases in depositions. I longed for courtroom trials.

It is a different career tactic to go from private firm to public servant. Most people in real life or on TV shows perform the reverse. They leap to the higher salary and grander décor.

When I arrived at the courthouse and adjoining District Attorney's office, not only was there no desk, there was nowhere for me to sit, except in an old conference room now used for storage. The District Attorney led me to the room with apologies as he pushed aside dusty files. He handed me a case to review before my first conference at 10:00 am and a day filled with meeting future friends - all good litigators and great people. I settled in, sipped a cup of coffee, and read through the documents, and then went to find a restroom.

The bathroom looked like it hadn't been touched since the building was constructed. Pale, small tiles. Tiny sinks. Narrow stalls. Staff, convicted criminals, witnesses, defendants out on bond, and defense attorneys all shared the same restrooms. No problem.

Dirty bars of soap blistered with bubbles from prior washes. Problem.

Yuck. I didn't want to complain on my first day. Besides, I was a tough girl from a small beach town. I didn't care about pretense. Shoot, I didn't often care about shoes, only the feel of sand or grass between my toes.

Apparently, I cared a lot about soap. I had to adapt. I worked late, met a lot of wonderful folks. By the end of the week, I brought in a case of Yardley pump soap. Long ago, my dad was the top salesman for Yardley of London. Lemon verbena and lavender were the scents of my childhood. Dad's Yardley career came and went before I arrived. Because it was a part of him, it was a part of me. I refilled the bathroom sinks and got to know the kind janitorial staff. Dad sent me perfumes and salt scrubs to share with my new friends. He, and they, lovingly teased me about cleaning up crime and bathrooms.

Soon, soap dispensers were installed. A sign of welcome at a job I loved.

A small change from posh to poignant work meant I had to choose whether to whine or happily solve. Choosing positivity made all the difference.

Years later, I found another affirming sign from a jar. At the office Christmas party, a one-gallon tub of mayonnaise had an upside-down plastic spork shoved in it for spreading. If soap meant I arrived, a gallon of mayo left out for hours and crowned with a spork meant it was time to go. While I had already considered moving into a private consulting role, the tub of mayo provided affirmation, as did friends who laughed and nodded with me.

Other times in life, I did not want to adapt. Dad advised, "Pick your battles." He forgot to add, "doing so is lonely." Sometimes our stubbornness to be right or be heard, results in others erecting walls.

We do not want to change. We want them to change.

They do not want to change. They do not see the need.

Quit pounding the wall. Fix what is in your control. Stop focusing on them and consider what is going on within. Is your persistence done with kindness or self-righteousness? Intent matters. And it can evolve. Focus less on the bad attitude of others and more on your positive pursuit. Affirm helpful people and forward steps. Build communities in lieu of burning bridges. Do not let the unyielding positions of others become an excuse for your anger or rudeness. As Mom always said, "There is never an excuse for rudeness."

As long as you are in your job, the job is never done.

The choice of how the job goes is yours.

People with a positive outlook choose joy. They claim it. Others observe and think it is innate, and while science says some inherently hold more joy than others, it is a pervasive, consistent choice to stay in light. Negative thoughts creep in everyone's head. Worry is our commonality. True grit enables us to transform pessimism and let it go. Working with negative people can pull you into darkness. This rarely happens in one swooping grasp. Cynicism is a harmful persistent bitterness, piercing our susceptible hearts. What's particularly tough to see are people who appear positive, but after partnering you soon discover their drive, integrity, and outlook are not what you expected. This can happen in friendships, marriage, and work. Do not let minor frustrations stew and brew. Address frustrations quickly by lovingly telling the truth or ignoring the nonsense. Paper cuts are not cause for combat. Love heals more than texts, memes or online rants and rage ever could. Get to the point of the pain and rely on listening as a vital tool to repair.

Many things need to be addressed, but all don't have to be addressed right now. We often get trapped in the oppression of the urgent. Others can encourage us to confront people or problems immediately.

"Oh, you should absolutely call her and tell her that was unacceptable."

"Do it!"

"I can't believe he said that. Text him back and tell him exactly how you feel. You are spot on."

"Do it!"

You hear the cheer of the crowd. They incite an urgency. With their nudging, you take an immediate stand, race to battle, then turn around to find those once beside you have taken two steps back or fled the scene.

Someone else's sense of urgency does not have to become your own.

Inhale love. Exhale your name.

Greek philosopher Epictetus wrote,
> *"The key is to keep company only with people who uplift you, whose presence calls forth your best."*

Easy if you own the business.

Hard if you are middle management.

Tough within a family.

If your reactions are not producing expected outcomes, change the influencers. If your current job brings you down, schedule time for healthy, positive pursuits. In lieu of meeting for coffee, ask a friend to meet for a walk or workout. Find groups who happily serve and join them. Expand your tribe. Build friendships, not networks. Collaborate in community. Hold each other up. Don't wait.

I know adding one more hour to your already crazed week may seem undoable. But of all places to enter, the most important is the sanctuary of your soul.

Reach out for help and look for ways to support others. Pain can be a pacifier, keeping us in a lonely, caustic cradle. Go beyond the comfort of constant. Get beyond yourself.

Surprise someone, even one who seems to have it all together, with your offer to help. Follow through. Maybe that person simply needs to know someone remembers a loss or a time when their work provided meaning. If a friend or co-worker loses a loved one and posts the obituary, read it. Learn from the summation of a life lived. Let those hurting know you see them, and they matter.

If the thought of someone brings you joy, tell them. Tell them while you can. Your reach out may be the difference between masterpiece and misery. Oh, for the joy of a shared smile on a pummeling day! We crave companionship. Whole-hearted living is a poignant, bold, necessary quest. Our souls long for relationships where we bear witness to each other's whole lives by loving one another as we are – beautifully made, broken, and bountiful.

If you want people to do the right thing, show them the right thing to do. Teenagers witness bad behavior and do not speak out. We wonder why they are silent and forget we never role-played scenarios or demonstrated ways to get help. We hire people, sure of their talents and then are surprised when they do not know how to communicate effectively via text, in person, and in large group settings. We *learn* best practices. People may intend to react in a positive way, but we all need reminders of how to constructively deal with frustration and fear. Fight or flight are not the only responses. Sometimes we freeze. We help people react wisely when we model expectations. Be what you wish to see. Be the friend, spouse, and co-worker you need right now.

With grit, we do unexpected, anonymous acts of grace and mercy.

With grit, we call somebody, invite them to dinner, show up on a door step or call with no agenda other than to "simply be."

For with grit, as the world swirls in colossal kindness and fracturing disarray, we rush to aid and honor. We get up when joy is boundless and again when we are tired - so tired and wondering what else to say. We go. In stillness, we know the good far outweighs any destruction.

Gritty warriors speak the truth, set boundaries, and come at people with love. They do not wait to meet in the middle. If I sit at a table of fools, grit arms me with knowing who I am. Nonsense doesn't shape me. Grit, grace, hope, and love hold the shield of integrity.

On my walks, runs, and sprints I pass a lot of wealth - families where generational money helps to purchase homes, pay for private schooling, and offer a safety net. On my best days, it is lovely. On my worst, it seems unfair. It is easy to assume their burdens are less than mine - leading to playing a game of "if only." The truth is everyone has weight to bear and burdens to carry.

Instead of becoming frustrated by what others have or the ways which it seems they are rescued with relief, we need to be still and recognize most trouble is temporary. Financial distress, strained relationships with family or friends, illness, and uncertainty are pains of life. With authentic grit, we allow stillness to ready us for the distance. In repeated quiet, mindful moments, gathering faith and garnering stillness, we find peace. No matter the circumstance, this continuous exercise empowers every one of us to declare, "it is well with my soul." But getting there takes practice.

Inhale self-confidence, exhale doubt.

Inhale faith, exhale fear.

Inhale love and all that is good, exhale your name.

Trust.

Stand with grit. Pour out the poisons preventing you from living your whole, abundant life. Pour in grit, grace, hope, and love.

Pour grit, grace, hope, and love on others.

Sometimes my pace is slow and my breathing labored. Sometimes my run is more like a dance.

Whatever my trot and lot, I press on.

The path you run is a road to history. It is your story. Your pains and joys. Your milestones and wandering in the wilderness. Your rest. Your sprint. Your crawl. Your stride. Your victory.

We need each other. We are not meant to strive alone.

Press on.

CHAPTER SEVEN

RESILIENCE

A song of the mighty.

Our oldest daughter, Cecily, has a beautiful voice. Each year her school puts on an elaborate musical production performed by the fifth grade. If you asked Cecily the summer before she entered fifth grade if she would try out for a part, she would politely say, "No." If we encouraged her by saying, "You have a beautiful gift to share," she might get red-eyed and then decline.

We knew she was nervous, scared, and unsure of her ability to carry off a solo. She sang for us. She sang with choirs. She recited speeches before large crowds. She did so on Christmas Eve in front of more than two thousand people. Cecily confidently walked to microphones with prepared words. We did not know why she feared singing a solo. She sings in our house and immediately brings soothing calm. It didn't make sense to us why she didn't want to share her gift, but it didn't really matter. It did not have to make sense. It simply was. Something made her no longer want to sing beyond our home. We loved her through it. We assured her things would be alright and, as she was ready, we talked with her about fears and overcoming them. Our job was to love. It was, and is, a joy to do so.

If Cecily never wanted to sing a solo, it was okay.

If she wanted to sing, but felt small, frozen, and terribly frightened, we stood with her to conquer.

Cecily's sister Gabrielle loves to sing and will do so on any occasion or field. One sister is not better or braver than the other. They love each other and encourage one another. They have different obstacles and ovations. We all do. Cecily has longed dreamed of being a surgeon. As a young girl, wound care and watching surgery videos are part of her joys and call. Her siblings encourage her while averting their gaze. They do not share her bravery in seeing blood.

For Cecily, fifth grade musical tryouts came in late winter. She decided to go ahead when she learned the initial tryouts were in a group format and solos were done one-on-one with the director. To my chagrin there were multiple call backs before handing out leads. She landed a role – an operatic chef. Practice after practice she diligently went, never singing a note in the car on the way home. As we neared opening night, friends and kids would come up to the car and exclaim,

"Cecily's voice is amazing."

"She holds this one long note so beautifully."

"She is strong. She's made for the stage."

All the while, Cecily asked us to wait until opening night to hear her. The show opened, she bounded out with all the other talented kids singing with the company. Then the time came for her solo.

Our friend Kenny offered to film the moment. In this incredible age of capturing every experience, I was awed by Kenny's thoughtful grace and presence of mind to empower us to just watch our daughter.

We did. She was amazing. Yes, I know I sound like every mom who ever posts or tweets. Cecily beautifully moved across the stage, each step purposefully and wonderfully timed with every word and note. A crescendo into the last part of her song made us hold our breath and then cry, "Wow!" She nailed it. Cecily lit up the stage and every Sully had tears in their eyes. We remembered when she once shook at the thought of performing. With perseverance, passion, and resilience, she found her home.

Kenny captured not just her voice; he panned over to us at the end of the song, cheering and tearing. Thank you to those who let us beautifully experience life unencumbered.

Cecily's powerful voice within her small frame is a call of the mighty. She found her song when she was ready. With practice and hard work, she persisted. She is resilient.

Resilience is strength emanating from broken places. It is the lifeblood of grit. It is a call of the mighty.

With resilience you are a conqueror, poet, and purveyor of love.

With resilience, your scars do not scare you; they remind you of strength and healing. Every touch point of life can push you down. Whole living begins when you decide to get back up.

Resilience is not about size or stature; it is the pliability inside. We are not going to let it destroy us, whatever *it* may be. Cancer, fired from a job and it makes headlines, a spouse cheats and the dream of a marriage dies, an ill and agitated shooter fires at innocent people, but we rise. The wounds may nearly break us. Resilience resides when we pull ourselves from the depth of obstacles *and* when we help others. We belong to each other. Stress, pain, and loss can flatten or fuel. We decide. To live fully and wholly is to experience stress, setbacks, and uncertainties. When hatred takes our breath away, resilience revives us with strength to love.

A childhood illness caused Helen Keller to become blind, mute, and deaf. Born into a different family, holding a different spirit of stubborn optimism, or never working with Annie Sullivan may have changed all Helen would become. A blind, mute, and deaf woman, born over one hundred years ago is the embodiment of resilience, the call of the mighty.

A young girl, no more than seven or eight years old, was raped by her mother's boyfriend. He was murdered soon thereafter. The girl had uttered his name and thought her voice caused his death. And so, she did not speak for many years, except to her brother Bailey. Already abandoned at age three by her mother and father, this little girl filled with fear from trauma, was smart, talented, and brave. She had a grandmother who gave her a home and told her she was worthy and loved. She found her voice. She studied, read, memorized, and wrote. She poured out her pain with honesty and reverence. She sang and danced. She became a professor, an innovator, and knew boredom meant life was over.

She believed she could continually begin again. In 1969, at the age of forty-one, Maya Angelou's book about her silence and overcoming was published. *I Know Why the Caged Bird Sings* explains the agony of bearing an untold story. Maya Angelou's life and body of work are the call of the mighty.

You are not Helen, Maya, Gabrielle or Cecily; you do not need to be. Your callings and obstacles are your own. You can become resilient. Get angry, not bitter. Use anger to lead you to acts of love, mercy, and justice. Get up. Push through. There is a beautiful untold story and song in you.

Relationships, reconciliation, and resilience.

I walked into our kids' bathroom this morning and found thirteen empty rolls of toilet paper. None left to spare. Where did it go? I was in this bathroom just yesterday having a discussion about replies. For example, the appropriate reply to the question - "Have you brushed your teeth?" – is not "Maybe" or "Almost." This was not a time for reckoning or reconciliation. It was simply time to close the door and tell the kids to clean.

Reconciliation is restoration. A cure found in secure places, the reconciling of us is where time and love join for healing. Reconciliation is where we shed rage and shame. We listen to pain. We use our anger. And as we do, through a community of grace, we find wholeness. We feel complete.

Reconciliation is the gift of wings. Truths unfold. Justice wraps with hope, and this clasp does not excuse what was done; it reconciles. Exposing awfulness is a risk as it may make things worse. Movies end, credits run, and we do not know what happens after the welcome home hug. A prodigal returns. Forgiveness is given. Life is renewed. We rejoice in a heralded story's end where the underdog shares success and finds reconciliation in a once torn relationship. Our view as the credits roll is typically of a joyful day one. By day three, laundry and dishes have piled up. By month three, irritation and stink can brew. We need reinforcement to continue reconciliation's work. Grit, grace, hope, and love sustain the restoration.

I have. I am. I can.

How we address adversity shapes our whole life. In *A Guide to Promoting Resilience in Children: Strengthening the Human Spirit*, Dr. Edith

Grotberg determined there are three sources for building resilient children called: *I HAVE, I AM, I CAN.*

Children draw from these three wells to overcome.

I HAVE:

- *People around me I trust and who love me, no matter what.*
- *People who set limits for me, so I know when to stop before there is danger or trouble.*
- *People who show me how to do things right by the way they do things.*
- *People who want me to learn to do things on my own.*
- *People who help care for me when I am sick, in danger or need to learn.*

I AM:

- *A person people can like and love.*
- *Glad to do nice things for others and show my concern.*
- *Respectful of myself and others.*
- *Willing to be responsible for what I do.*
- *Sure things will be alright.*

I CAN:

- *Talk to others about things that frighten me or bother me.*
- *Find ways to solve problems that I face.*
- *Control myself when I feel like doing something not right or dangerous.*
- *Figure out when it is good time to talk to someone or to take action.*
- *Find someone to help me when I need it.*

Adversity is universal; none of us are exempt. We do not need all the *I HAVE, I AM, I CAN* tools, but one is not enough.

I asked our youngest, Gabrielle, to read this list. She said,

"I like it. It's a good list. I have trouble with 'I can.'"

"Why?" I asked.

"Because sometimes it's hard to stop doing something not right or dangerous. I'm a ninja architect."

She is an honest, insightful ninja architect.

Resilience is a roar.

Benjamin Waterhouse Hopkins was a sculptor, illustrator, and artist with a passion for natural history. He studied dinosaurs. In the 1850s few people knew what dinosaurs might look like. There were fossils and bits and pieces, but nothing to scale. Hopkins brought dinosaurs to life. Like anyone who creates and exhibits, he faced critics. He worried about England's leading scientists approving his gigantic models. To gain their support, he invited them to a formal dinner on New Year's Eve. The table set, footmen at the ready, courses and wines paired. His guests arrived, climbed the steps, and passed through heavy drapes to find their seat inside an iguanodon. To bring them in, Benjamin Waterhouse brought his guests *inside*.

In our pursuits of purpose and passion, we often want approval, but are reticent to let people in.

A life interrupted is one well lived. While focusing on our visions, we can miss opportunities. With your head face down in a phone, an untapped dream tugs at your sleeve.

Look up. Listen. It is the call of the mighty.

An invitation awaits to dine with dinosaurs – a roar of tenacity and imagination.

How will you reply?

Resilience = Optimism + Overcoming.

One of the most common links shared among Fortune 100 CEOs is dyslexia.

It is estimated that twenty percent of the global population, approximately one-in-five people, are dyslexic. Commonly viewed as a reading issue with kids turning letters backwards, it is, in fact, a deeper, richer neurological distinction. Dyslexics have a learning difference providing significant cognitive advantages. Dyslexia offers alternative processing pathways empowering innovative, non-linear, creative thinking. Dyslexics have the unique ability to observe a situation or circumstance and recognize solutions others cannot see. What might appear to most as a discord of disparate pieces, dyslexics find connections that others overlook.

Dyslexics represent a significant percentage of all self-made millionaires and scientists. Sociologists, such as Julie Logan of the Cass Business School in London, have found dyslexia is common among entrepreneurs as they are people who view the big picture and analyze creatively.

My husband is dyslexic, and one of our children is dyslexic. Sully did not know he was dyslexic until our oldest son, Jack, was tested. This is a common tale as dyslexia can be mild, moderate or severe. We have Jack's permission to share this small piece of his astounding, continuing story. Jack did well in elementary school. There were little signs. He did not cross mid-line but instead would begin writing an answer in the middle of the page. He would skip words when reading but could mask the omission by filling in the gaps with his own intellect and summation. His strengths in memorization and oration have always been far beyond his years. He lovingly, persuasively commands a room with strength, grace, and compassion. The parts of his beautiful mind causing difficulty in spelling are the components of warrior poets and corporate giants.

> *Pablo Picasso, Alexander Graham Bell, Wolfgang Amadeus Mozart, John Irving, Benjamin Franklin, Mohammed Ali, Leonardo da Vinci, Pierre Curie, Carol Greider, Agatha Christie, William Butler Yeats, Winston Churchill, Thomas Jefferson, Maggie Aderin-Pocock, Dav Pilkey, Jennifer Aniston, Keira Knightly, Tim Tebow, Ingvar Kamprad, Tommy Hilfiger, Charles Schwab, Steven Spielberg, Whoopi Goldberg, Barbara Corcoran, Kevin O'Leary, Daymond John, John Chambers, David Mc-Comas, Bill Hewlett, Helen B. Taussig, George Clooney, Anderson Cooper, Erin Brockovich, Paul Orfalea, Orville Wright, Wilbur Wright, Phillip Schultz, and ....*

The list of incredible achievers who share in the dyslexia blessings is long and wondrous. Renowned cardiologists, Nobel Prize winners, artists, award winning writers, athletes, actors, entrepreneurs, and pioneers in science, mathematics, architecture, and movies all share this gift. At first, I was worried for my child. With research, I saw the wonder.

Every one of us, for all our whole, beautiful, imperfect lives, is overcoming.

Overcoming is part of becoming all you are called to be.

Resilience demands patience for the good to unfold. No matter the discouragement, believe in the present beauty and in the wonder to come.

"Being dyslexic is actually an advantage…
The world is made by dyslexia."
- SIR RICHARD BRANSON, FOUNDER, THE VIRGIN GROUP

"Dyslexia made me stronger. Struggle can be good. Chal-
lenges can make us better. People who must overcome
difficulties often have a greater determination to succeed
in work and life. I know this firsthand; it wasn't until I
was 35 years old and a practicing cardiac surgeon that I
got a name for why my education had been so difficult:
dyslexia."
-TOBY COSGROVE, M.D.

CEO AND PRESIDENT, THE CLEVELAND CLINIC

"This is who I am."
- GARY COHN, FORMER PRESIDENT AND CHIEF OPERATING
OFFICER, GOLDMAN SACHS

You don't have to wait on a dream. Go get it.
Anything and everything are possible
with this awesome gift.
- JACK SULLIVAN, INTERNATIONAL BACCALAUREATE®
HONORS STUDENT, MULTI-SPORT VARSITY ATHLETE, AND
DEBATE TEAM CAPTAIN

  Dyslexics make exceptional astrophysicists because they can detect star patterns others cannot see.

When one of our children is tired or weary, maybe even tearful after a long, trying day, we sit by their bed and remind them of their gifts.

We hold them, look them in the eye and say, *"Sweetie, you can do this. You are a conqueror. You have gifts far beyond what you can imagine. You are called to discover stars that others cannot see."*

Our prayer and advocacy are for educational systems where teachers and resources abound to help all students find their stars.

We believe in this pursuit. It is not easy. I litigate and advocate, not with a scorched earth approach, but in the determined challenge of leading with love. I don't always do it well, for seeing kids denied basic accommodations or retaliated against can raise my ire. "Lazy," "stupid," and "unfocused" - these are the names called. Or worse, they are unseen. Sitting in a classroom, not failing or excelling, these students are underperforming because of rote methodologies offering a one-size-fits-all. Our goal is teaching children self-advocacy. "Build your case" is a mantra we repeat. "Give voice to the voiceless with kindness and love," is a reminder to all. Along the way, we encounter thought leaders, teachers, and friends who fill us and tend to our fatigue. We join them and press on.

With a significant number of the United States' prison population having learning disabilities, there is the potential for building future entrepreneurs, artists, innovators, scientists, lawyers and the like, in lieu of a life stifled behind bars. We must believe in providing individual learning plans suited for seeing and capturing stars, instead of containing capacity.

Empathy.

To love people is to see them from the inside out. Treating people with dignity and respect is helpful in healthcare and at gas stations. We honor one another when we see each other through a lens of love.

On a trip to the beach we stopped at a gas station in Alabama. It was on a street lined with historic homes featured in paintings, books, magazines, and movies. All four kids were excited as we promised they each could pick one snack to buy. Entering the station, we saw a biker clad in jeans, a leather vest, with an American flag bandana tied around his head. He held the door open for us, and our three-year-old daughter Gabrielle wanted to acknowledge her new friend.

As he said, "Afternoon, ma'am," she looked up, stared into his eyes and full beard and loudly said,

"Thank you, pirate."

I don't remember what Gabrielle chose as snack that day. I just remember holding in laughter and hoping she did not offend the biker.

Maybe he was a pirate, for he didn't scoff or scold.

He said, "Argh! You are so welcome."

I do remember her then five-year-old sister Cecily excitedly getting a pack of gum for her treat. Back in the car and twenty miles down the road, I asked the kids to hand up their trash. Up came wrappers from a candy bar, chips, and gum. There were lots and lots of gum wrappers. Cecily wasn't blowing a massive bubble. She had eaten fifteen pieces for her snack. She saved three for her siblings. I suppose the bright side is she looked beyond herself.

For resilience to take hold, your focus should extend beyond yourself. Resilient people are empathetic and optimistic. They see the good. They trust, pursue passions, instill hope in others, and have a community of support. It is much of what you see on *Sesame Street*.

Sesame Workshop®, the non-profit educational arm behind the long running television show, *Sesame Street*, conducted a survey encompassing kindness and empathy. The ability to understand, identify with, and share the feelings of another, *empathy* is more than walking in someone else's shoes. It is sensing someone's emotions, along with grasping their thoughts or feelings and experiences.

With sympathy, we "feel for" and in empathy we "feel with." They are skills we can develop.

With empathy, we expand the quality of our relationships ahead of the quantity. Empathy allows us to develop deeper, more meaningful connections, for with empathy we foster compassion and care. An empathic person loves his neighbor. Empathy comes in the middle of the night to watch your children as you head to the hospital. It is listening and staying without knowing or curing. Empathy understands powerlessness.

With empathy, a mere object becomes a work of art.

In the Sesame Workshop study, they found an overwhelming seventy percent of parents believe the world is an unkind place. Kindness is needed, and its absence causes concern. The survey included several potential descriptors of kindness including: empathy, helpfulness, thoughtfulness, and manners.

It turns out manners were most important to parents. When parents were asked to choose between manners and empathy, then decide which was more important for their child to hold right now, fifty-eight percent chose manners.

When teachers were asked the same question of their students, seventy-one percent chose empathy. The gap is significant. Some parents may perceive teaching manners builds empathy, but there is no research to support this contention. You can have exceptional manners and be completely self-absorbed. Bullies tend to mask their meanness with manners. Remember the Eddie Haskell character in *Leave It To Beaver* or any mean girl in high school who is polite to adults while terrorizing peers or singling out one in particular? Tina Fey luminously captures the skills of faked niceties while plotting destruction in her movie and musical, *Mean Girls*.

Good manners are an important way of honoring each other. However, we must be careful not to elevate their usefulness beyond the bountiful gifts of empathy.

Resilient, gritty, whole people are empathetic. They serve in community, recognize the emotional needs of others, and believe they will see good work to conclusion. They move beyond manners to deeper, relational connections. They do not develop empathy in isolation. They couple empathy with concern, compassion, and loving-kindness. They are willing to do the right, hard, best thing because they believe in the greater good, the pinnacle pursuit. They believe they can overcome obstacles arising on the journey. They believe in improving the lives of others. They are reflective, internally considering if their words and actions will hurt or heal.

It is easier to have empathy for like-minded people. We are quick to insult strangers whose circumstances we know nothing about. True grit, resilience, and whole living require understanding the importance of empathizing with people who are different. But different doesn't have to be distant.

Life is full of circumstances I cannot change. What I can control is my reply.

Our son Henry asked this morning, "Mom, can you solve an equation?"

I smiled and answered, "That's a pretty broad question. You didn't say what type or when, but my answer is, 'Yes.'"

I don't know if I can immediately solve his equation, but together we can learn how to solve it. We are capable. Our energy and creativity will determine the outcome.

Build a legacy of resilience, grit, grace, hope, and love or forfeit whole lives; think about where you are today. Are you having a bad season or are you milking one bad game? Is it a horrible year or are some obstacles arising amongst miracles? Is it a rough day or one brief irritating moment you let simmer all day?

Situations and conditions do not have to define your destiny.

When Henry was seven, he played little league. It is the stage where young boys become mighty giants as they run on the field while you can still see the images of super hero underwear through their white pants. Parents are on the field to cheer and guide as all look for the ball and a place to stand or run. Henry's team lost every single game. On more than one occasion, the referees invoked the "mercy rule," so the opposing team's gains were not added to the scoreboard blowout. At the end of the season, other teams heard of our losing streak and would still bring cowbells and cartwheeling sisters to holler at the slaughter. Our boys did not lose hope. They got up and tried in every play. One grand-pa was integral in prodding them along. Whenever we got a bit of a run or movement toward a triumph, he would yell, "Take it to the barn!"

With his deep call and a circling tight fist, his cheer echoed a never give up alarm to drown out the whistles of fear.

"Take it to the barn!"

He believed they could.

I need to hear him shouting this now. It's 11:48 pm and I must wrap up writing and prepare for the tooth fairy. A colorful note resting near the tooth placed deep underneath a pillow requests fairy dust, a feather, and an explanation for what the tooth fairy does with all the teeth.

There is a job to do and doing it well will make all the difference to someone I love. No matter my exhaustion or search for feathers and loose change, I must "Take it to the barn!"

I need to hear it as I read more about the concerns of safety with little league sports and finding healthy outlets for exercise and team building. Parenting is a mine field of worry with watchful admonitions from researchers and moms with high cheekbones, furrowless foreheads, and leggings awesomely accentuating a post-Pilates workout. These women are readied with wine in stainless steel tumblers, bottles of electrolyte water, and gourmet snacks for long evenings on the ball field, while I hold a cold venti coffee I never finished hours earlier.

"Take it to the barn!"

We all need this axiom.

Your beautiful, whole life awaits.

Resilience is our relentless hope.

Together, let's join the call of the mighty.

CHAPTER EIGHT

COURAGE

In 1989, a bull became a landmark in South Manhattan. Artist Arturo Di Modica designed *Charging Bull* - a formidable, iconic statue and symbol of Wall Street. Typifying relentless strength, the bull is in motion without barrier, boundary, or opponent. Tail wound like a whip. Rippling muscles. Menacing eyes. Legs tightened, body leaning and ready to strike. Tourists stop to take pictures, grabbing the horns, marking a memory of their trek to a monument where fortunes flourish and markets prevail. The fluidity of the statue exudes courage even if economies weaken. The bull stands alone.

That is until March 2017, when State Street Global Advisors installed a statue of a little girl. She stands with fists on hips perhaps giving a direction, adversary or interruption to the bull's intent. Her hair and dress are blown, without certainty if by the storms of life or the flaring nostrils and battle hungry breath of a raging bull.

This young girl faced the giant. The bull, once charging against the world without a singular opponent, found a lowly, fragile foe. Or so it seemed. The bull is a beautiful, enormous locomotion. A sure-footed little girl surprises us and the beast. She is battle ready. Her shoes are tightly laced, ankles and heels covered. Legs protected with pants seeming more like leggings or stockings, easily torn. A simple dress. No bows of any kind. Her hair is tightly tied back. It is smooth on top and bound in a ponytail so no strands blow in her face. Her eyes are open and directly squared on her opponent.

She brings all she has to battle - her intellect, resolve, fortitude, faith, and bravery - for they are all she needs. She is not weighed down by another's armor or their perceptions of what she needs to triumph. Winning is defined on her terms, for she is victorious the moment she stands. Prevailing against such a foe may include a fall and the need to bounce back. Success might require a series of stands. Unlike David's long told walk to Goliath, there is no bag of stones. But maybe she knows the stones never belonged to David. They were not his source of strength. His courage began within.

Slaying giants.

Stature shows strength. This tiny girl stands tall amongst mighty Wall Street towers. Her fortification is a super hero stance. Arguably, merely holding this pose shores up her courage. Fists on hips is intentional. She is strengthening her core, lifting her chest, her center of truth. Her feet firmly planted. This positioning immediately helps her withstand initial blows, even those of uncertainty coming from within.

The strength of her stance demonstrates wisdom. For if a little girl places herself boldly in the path of a raging bull, looking him squarely in the eye, she must know something we do not know. She must see what our eyes fail to view. As of now, she stands unaccompanied and unaided. Those who might race to stand with her are inspired by her courage or fear her fate. Maybe a courageous soul might want to scoop her up and release her from danger, but her stance conveys she does not need rescuing. She is equipped to liberate herself and ultimately help others break free.

Her posture and presence may change our view of heroes and bulls. The bull's head pulled to the right and his arched brows could infer curiosity and surprise for what hails ahead. A firm, hard tail whirling above is perhaps vacillating between recoil and ravage. Three hoofs planted with one in motion to ready the charge are now possibly applying brakes to wonder about this little girl who dares to courageously remain.

The Fearless Girl is designed by artist, Kristen Visbal. Why is she fearless? Maybe *fearless* depicts her stance and not her heart and head. Courageous people seem fearless. She looks fearless, but we cannot see inside. We perceive courage is walking bravely, without fear. And yet, with courage, we go, no matter the internal fear or trembling. As Mark Twain explained, "Courage is resistance to fear, mastery of fear – not absence of fear." No matter her name or title, this little girl is courageous. It takes courage to stand.

She is brave. She is alone. She may be the only person who knows she is afraid. Bravery dwells in unexpected places.

Her courage combines with hope and faith. Like first responders who race upward when others head down, courage acts in the face of fear. The danger is ahead, and while most run to safety, the courageous march forward. They honor. They listen. They seek wisdom and pursue justice. They stand, walk humbly, and race to rescue, stamping out danger, soothing wounds, and abating harm. Courage is the work of the strong and the weary. Passion pulsates in courage. It takes courage to endure pain, whether inflicted by a knife or a callous voice. It takes courage to discover who you are rather than floating through life unaware of intimacy, others, and unfulfilled wholeness.

The Fearless Girl focuses on what is in front of her. While added foes may arise, she addresses what is ahead. She does not let herself stray off course by anything shiny or scary on the periphery.

Her stance is not without controversy. Is State Street's statue a push for gender parity or a public relations precursor to paying millions to women and minorities who worked at the firm? Art evokes pain, possibility, and interpretation. Van Gogh's strokes captured brilliance, isolation, and mental illness. Manet and Goya's nudes depicted truths, shocking initial viewers. Art impacts and imparts long after the reasons for instillation, for art and life are dynamic, fluid, still, and erupting.

Arguments arose contending *The Fearless Girl* unduly interrupted *Charging Bull* by merging two distinct pieces of art into one. Did *The Fearless Girl* trespass? Were the bull and the girl single installments, each looking to the open horizon without parameters? Or, did they fully encompass one another, with a view only of girl to bull and bull to girl? Both ignite passion.

And why install a statue of a little girl? Why not erect a warrior woman facing the bull?

Even when the bull stood alone, tourists and passersby placed themselves in front of him. People temporarily filled the girl's space until she arrived. Did they see themselves as the bull's opponent? Or does the bull represent all of us against an uncertain world?

Is the girl a façade or bearer of truth? After all, none of us is perfectly self-sufficient. We stand broken, scarred, and worried. We are wobbly even when our stance seems sure. Yet it is within this authenticity and fragility where love does its best work.

Maybe we view giant beasts as ones who win, when who we should see and be is the little girl. Her enormous courage outweighs the bull's massive size. To live an abundant, whole life, we must look beyond norms of anticipated winners and losers. We need to see ourselves as vulnerable, complex, uncertain, beautiful, worthy, wounded warriors who conquer with our weaknesses.

What is inside determines outcomes.

She is the victor the moment she stands.

Time, courts, politicians, and pundits determine how long and where she stays. The girl has already been moved once. Her new home resides about three blocks away, outside the stock exchange and facing the building. Spectators still come to see both. They tug the bull's horns. Replicate her pose. And take selfies. Do they wonder what will become of the two? Perhaps these adversaries will morph into allies. She will run with the bull and he will run with her. Not every day, all day, for each must take their own path and champion their callings. How brave to be different yet be in life together.

Someday, the bull may represent boldness becoming her friend. For underneath all the muscle and mass rests fear and self-doubt, wrestling with passion and purpose.

You are courageous.

You are a mighty bull. You are a courageous child.

You are braver than you can imagine. Stop. Wade into these words. Do not rush through this message as a blithe statement applying to others. Hold this truth. You are full of vigor and zest. There is unmet boldness within you.

Alone, ground shaking whether from thundering, roaring lions, earthquakes or a doctor's dire prognosis, courage stands. Courage says let's solve, fight, and conquer in truth and love.

We are wired for meaningful belonging.

Courage unfolds when you are in a community who calls it out, cheers it on, and pushes you onward. You rise and others are there to sturdy your gait when you falter. They are not insecure or jealous because of your growing courage. It is fostered, honored, and honed. It is where you grow into your whole, full life because you help others stand, and it brings you joy to do so. No likes, hashtags or posts needed. You are filled in their becoming and in your serving and support, whether seen or unrecognized.

Our call for companionship.

A whole, abundant, thriving community:
1. Hears you.
2. Needs you.
3. Carries you.

1. Hears you.

Some religious organizations have annual celebrations to impart blessings on animals. You can carry your animal (dogs, cats, birds, geckos, bunnies, snakes – which is not likely preferred or recommended to be seated next to said bunny) down the church aisle and receive a prayer. Many enjoy this ritual. I avoided it for years, but, alas, as my kids grew older and wiser, they begged to bring our Great Dane and Black Lab to the service. Our Great Dane refused into get the car, and so we headed off with only Reagan Batman Sullivan. Really, what else would you call a Black Lab?

We walked in, all four kids and one dog in tow, and the kids begged for front row seating. I soon learned it is easy to find frustration and a short fuse in a long church pew. Reagan Batman charged after several curious creatures. He wanted to lick or sniff every animal headed up for a blessing. I thought the prayer service would be an in-and-out process and didn't realize there was also hymn singing and a short message. Barking, crying, pee and other fluids puddling on floors and soaking hand-stitched cushions - my kids loved it. My husband laughed. He patted my back knowing I did not want one more wet nose or butt stuck in my face. I love animals, but this was overload. Some creatures were huge and I was on the aisle with a dog and two kids on my lap. I shuffled down the pew to get out of pet love range. I looked around to see if others shared my longing for the whole ordeal to be over.

I saw her. An elderly friend with a smile you hope every wonderful grandmother carries. She mouthed, "Hello." I could hear it. It was as if she said, "It's okay. It will be over soon, and you get can get outside on the lawn where you and the animals can roam." I occasionally teach a class this lady attends. It is filled with men and women her age. They sing songs before we begin. We talk about work to be done. Wrinkles, hunched backs, aches, oxygen tanks, and walkers often cause us to look solely at a life lived. I love asking about their hopes, dreams, quests – their "to be." I know their beautiful, unique journey is not done. There is air in their lungs. With breath, we are called to bring out light and life in each other.

My friend delights. She encourages me to wear high heels for as long as possible before my fashion is dictated by sensibility and orthopedic prescription. She sat five or six rows behind us. In the middle of the animal procession, I lifted my leg high to show her my ankle strapped heels. My friend didn't shake her head and admonish. She could have, after all she is old and perhaps that translates to "proper." She smiled and then surprised me. Like a Rockette stretching before high kicks and a step ball change, she quickly shot up her pant leg and showed me her black orthopedic Mary Janes. We saw each other. We heard one another. I awed in her dexterity. We were silly in a church service and shared our secret knowing with affirming nods.

Animals, kids, songs, prayers, and high kicks move us. They all have influence, and if you are lucky, they will converge in one sitting.

2. Needs you.

At a closed meeting to discuss Atlanta's crime rate and poverty, several community leaders allowed cameras and reporters to listen before they convened for a justice forum. Men and women were seated around a large table. Ambassador Andrew Young raised his hand to speak. In Atlanta, Ambassador Andrew Young did not need to raise his hand to have the floor. He offered humility and grace in his brave words. With a gentle voice, he spoke of our need to care for each other:

> *"We have mental problems, anxiety problems and economic problems. The only attitude we can have is how we pastor."*

"Pastor" comes from the Latin term meaning "to shepherd." A whole, blooming community is one where we pastor each other. We watch over, nurture, feed, guide, and offer counsel and consequences. It is hard work requiring wisdom, discipline, patience, humility, grit, grace, hope, and love. We admit wrongdoings and grow in gentleness, kindness, and compassion. We serve in our best capacity when it is not done for ego, but because of an inherent belief to bring light and a call to make a difference.

3. Carries you.

A Fortune 100 Company is struggling and cannot understand why. Quarterly earnings are not optimal, but they are up. Retention is average. Attrition is slightly above-average, but not enough to cause alarm. There are metrics the C-suite can see, but they miss what matters. The employees are not carrying each other. This state of business led to mistrust, insecurity, and over-inflated self-promotion. A team manager describes it best:

> *"We're all in one boat trying to reach the shore. One is working on a faulty rudder, others have oars and are paddling hard, while some offer the same energy using only their hands. We're racing against different vessels. We have a shared goal. Our joint effort gets us to our destination, but the only one who gets the praise is the one who touches the shore first. It doesn't matter if heavy lifting came from the back of the boat."*

Create an atmosphere of "me, myself, and I" and the focus will always be on "me, myself, and I."

People who thrive on animosity, conspiracy, and over-confidence, captivate. Angry crowds act and vote. Have courage. Have the courage to lead in love. Stir up a mixture of graciousness and goodwill. Set alight "us" and "we" without demeaning "them." Find common whole-hearted goals instead of shared enemies.

Courage comes in the quiet as well as in the storm.

Courageously carrying each other out of foxholes, loneliness, and negativity and into sanctuaries of grace is where we do our most important work. It is an extension of love. A bomb goes off and people shelter in place. Stores close and become a respite for the injured and weary. Hospitals and rescue workers arrive, even if they are not on call. Being there is everything.

How do we reach the holed up? How do we make ourselves whole?

Mister Rogers' mother told him to look for the helpers in times of trouble. Whole, abundant, thriving communities raise helpers.

What If?

Lately I've had a mindset shift during my travels to and from sports fields.

I think of my parents. My dad had a football scholarship to Wabash College. He played on an undefeated team and became captain his senior year. In four years on the field, no one in his family ever watched him play. My mom's mother died when she was young. Her father, debilitated by depression was present, but absent. He did not walk her to school, attend plays, or ensure she was tucked in at night. She raised herself and her younger brother. My mother is deaf in one ear because of lack of proper medical care as a child. No parent ever cheered her on from the bleachers. I remember this often when we cheer for her namesake – our Cecily. We talk, laugh, and sing with perspiring, rowdy kids in the car and I realize these journeys are fleeting. Mud, stink, tired bodies, frustration from bad calls, and collections of weeds deemed floral bouquets by our youngest are all part of the beauty. I realize it is good, hard, stunning, and temporary.

My second shift is exercising while the kids are on fields. Instead of sitting in the car working, standing on the sidelines and catching up with parents or getting comfortable in a collapsible chair that expands into a throne resembling my dad's favorite recliner but with the added protection of a sun blocking canopy, I encourage a walk or a run. Sometimes a friend joins me or I get precious one-on-one time with one of our four. We cheer as we go, watching practice, exercising, and sharing life.

Occasionally cases interfere. I let the ostensible urgency get in the way of time to reset and connect. Recently I sat in my car working on an email reply to clients who were hurting. As I sat frustrated for them, building a substantive argument and remedy, hope knocked on the window. Our beloved friend and pediatrician, Shea, could tell my mind and heart were heavy.

We spoke about advocacy for children. She said,

> *"What if all the hard work and law school debt was for this moment? What if it was just for the work you've done for your own kids and other children? Wouldn't it be worth it?"*

Her wisdom came from searching this question long ago. What if all the medical school bills and hours were for one saved life? The moment an injured child begins breathing again, the rallying reply is, "Of course, it was all worth it. It was all for this."

We move on from rescuing. We forget what and who we bring back to life.

What if?

Two words changed my outlook. The work still had to be done, life's struggles did not disappear, but I gained courage through a different perspective. I did not do it alone.

What if it was all for this?

Healing happens in closed rooms with sick patients and though car windows.

Living a full, whole life - as you are, broken and becoming, holed and healing - is courageous. *What ifs* are your wings.

Combat fatigue.

Years ago, I had a difficult business decision to make. I wanted to leave a current role. It was the job I had once longed for, prayed for, and received. I sought insight and counsel from trusted friends. What prevented me from moving forward in my dreams? Fear – only I did not recognize it as fear. My hurdle was not the anticipation of conversations with colleagues. It was the fall-out.

Fear drives self-fulfilling prophecies. I had to become honest with myself about the cost. I had to speak out my resistance to understand why I stayed instead of getting free.

What once was wonderful, became weird and broken. I didn't know how to fix it or fix me.

Here's what I knew:

- Getting free is hard. Peace comes with mini-flares of misgivings. We all have them. To break free, acknowledge the fear. Transform worry into a statement of hope. *"What if this pain leads to a magnificent adventure?"*
- Don't just ponder your dream. Go.

- Living a whole life requires break-ups and make-ups. Not every job is ideal. Not every friendship will bloom. Mourn the loss. Speak the pain and remember failures fade. Grit, grace, hope, and love ignite dreams.

Here's what I wanted:

- To lead with love and leave with love. I didn't need acknowledgement of any wrongdoings. Alright, I admit that would be nice, but it wasn't going to happen. I wanted to take the next role. I wanted to shape the transition narrative, knowing in the end it was largely out of my control. I wanted to give grace and receive it. And, I wanted to let go of pain.

Here's what I learned:

- Listen to the nudge within. Trust yourself when you are swimming in grit, grace, hope, and love.
- Determine what your soul desires instead of what the outside world demands.
- Stop magnifying lack and minimizing bounty.
- Sit in the quiet and allow time to meditate in truth. Be stronger than your ego. Assess possibilities and support for when things get hard and go awry. Prepare for conversations. Have meaningful talks.
- Bear good fruit. Remember the words of Saint Basil, "A tree is known by its fruit; a man by his deeds. A good deed is never lost; he who sows courtesy reaps friendship, and he who plants kindness gathers love."

- Say "yes" to joy and outrageous dreams.
- You can assume the best while readying for pain. Your plan will likely change. As my friend Rebecca says, "You can only control the controllables," and little is controllable except your reply.
- Jumping off is scary and exhilarating. You hope for a soft landing, but sometimes there is an aching second bounce. To try anything new, you must let go. It is worth the leap, even with a rough start. Eventually, you will stick the landing.

Go ahead and jump!

Each of our children is brave in their own beautiful ways. So are you.

Our eldest daughter, Cecily, is wise and courageous. She is attuned to others and brings laughter and healing. She is hard on herself and sets high expectations on sports fields and in coursework. In doing so, she remarkably maintains her joy.

A year and a half ago, friends invited us to their lake home. At one point, everyone jumped off the boat house into the dark, cold water. It took Cecily a long time to decide whether or not to jump. She got all the way to the top of the boat house, held her dad's hand, but did not leap. We told her we were just as proud of her decision to look down and choose not to jump. She became quiet. We waited. She was terrified. Shaking. My heart ached and raced for her, but we let her do this at her own pace, on her own time. Wide eyes and legs going back and forth over the railing, she made the choice. It was okay to eventually head back down. Jumping did not define her. Neither did fear. We told her we loved her no matter if she walked down or flew. Then we gave her space to decide.

With a nod, a soft smile and arms open, she leapt.

Jump. It may sting. You may pull yourself up the ladder on to the dock, and gracelessly pull out a painful wedge caused by a bathing suit bunched in your behind. Everyone does this at one time or another – vacillates on what to do and yanks out wedgies. None of it should ever make you feel less than.

Deciding not to jump is as powerful as deciding to leap. Tell your stories of when you jumped and when you opted to stay still, remain anchored, or go home.

One time my church youth group went to a water park. On the ride over everyone excitedly discussed the new Kamikaze fall. The name of the ride could have been Turbo Death Wish or Slide of Satan. It was steeper and scarier than anything else in the park. We hurried through the turnstiles, got our mats, and ascended the stairs to the fall. I reached the top, with friends in front of me and behind. The drop looked so steep; I could not see what could stop me from flipping forward and hurdling down the slide ending with a crash landing. My turn came. I put my mat down in the tiny wading area before my descent into death, or at least a sixth-grade perception of a fatal journey. The life guard commanded, "Go." I stayed. I looked down. It was steep, vertical, and very, very far. He might have uttered encouraging words. My friends may have nudged or teased. I don't remember. I looked out over the water park and all there was to do. I didn't have to do this. I picked up my mat and walked back down.

I broke free.

Freedom is the key to allowing your soul to become all it can be.

Believe, even in the presence of fear. Believe love is on the horizon. It is. It may be a long way off, but good will come. Often it comes running.

Love is courageous.

Love runs to you and calls you by name.

On a crisp, sunny late February afternoon, we were outside watching our kids ride bikes and run around in the yard. Our youngest son, Henry, was riding his bicycle with his sister Cecily, while our youngest, Gabrielle, played in the yard. They like to ride down our next-door neighbor's driveway. It has a slight decline, giving a brief acceleration before reaching the garage door. Small trees separate our yards preventing us from seeing the entire driveway. We talked with friends, laughing as we described Henry's portrayal of Teddy Roosevelt earlier that morning at school. His handle bar moustache was reminiscent of my dad and old portraits of men clinking steins. It was a beautiful, blue sky day.

We didn't hear the crash. Screams and Henry's anguished cry broke through our conversation. Henry had peddled down our neighbor's driveway and crashed through the glass windows in the garage door. You would expect injuries on his forearms. A protective instinct is to duck and cover. He had extensive, deep bilateral lacerations extending from inside both hands to his upper arms, slicing them open down to fascia and bone. We heard his screams and rushed to him. We didn't know what we would find. As we ran, we saw Henry running to us in shock. He now had one shoe on. With terrified, painful cries his arms were open to us, but they didn't look like his arms any more.

In the movies, tragedy is sometimes enacted not in the bloodied bodies, but in the horror etched on faces. When I imagine the accident, I see his terrified face before I see his wounds. Henry ran to us with his skin and muscle torn apart and hanging off the lengths of both arms and hands - exposed, filleted open, and blood gushing everywhere.

Friends scooped up our daughters so they would not see the trauma. My husband tore his shirt and made tourniquets as he called for me to run inside and get Henry's belts, quickly thinking their small size may help stop the bleeding. We worked to keep Henry conscious. Police came. The fire department showed up. Ladder 26 kept him stable. Then the ambulance arrived to rush our baby boy to Children's Healthcare of Atlanta.

He suffered severe nerve and tendon damage. As his surgeon later told us, "He is a miracle." Henry's healing and recovery took a long time. He missed many weeks of school.

To return to his classroom, we had to ensure someone could help him in class and use the restroom. Some leaders were wonderful. Others had no plan. We had to choose whether to proceed with courage or keep our son home for the remainder of the year.

Peter, an assistant principal we love encouraged us to come to school for an hour with Henry so we could assess his needs and develop solutions together. We arrived, pulled the car to the curb, and helped our son out of the car. Nervous, worried, concerned.

A long way off, far beyond the school front door, deep in the ball field, beyond the playground, we heard someone calling his name. From a long way off, his former kindergarten teacher, Jake, a handsome, thoughtful, smart, kind man with a warm smile, let go of his task and called our son's name. Jake called and then he ran.

"Henry, Henry, Henry!"

He called and he ran with his arms wide open. He carried no worry of how he might hug a heavily bandaged and bruised boy.

From a long way off, he called our son by name. He ran and arrived with tears and welcome. He believed in all that is possible, and he stood with us with love and gratitude.

From a long way off, he brought courage, strength, and goodness.

From a long way off, he told Henry he was worthy and loved.

From a long way off, he assured us we were not alone.

This child could not yet hold a pen or a ball, but with courage he could stand.

Boldly go.

Words are powerful; they matter. We know this precept and often ignore it with all we let inside. We become what we say we are. We become what others say we are.

Our daughter Gabrielle is in an after-school running program for conditioning, training, and strengthening. At nine, she is the best runner in our family because she runs onward, regardless of the hill ahead. Not long ago, I picked up Gabrielle from her stint. She got in the car, we shared hellos, smiled, and then the car was quiet. I looked in rear view mirror and saw one tear rolling down her cheek. I asked, "Sweetie, what's wrong?"

"I'm mad," she said.

"Mad at whom?" I asked.

"At me."

"And insecure boys."

Ooh, this got interesting. There's a story to tell. She explained everyone was running the track determining times for completing a mile. She was not happy with her time and muttered to herself. A boy asked what she said. She replied expressing her frustration and telling him her time. He laughed. Told her she wasn't just slow. She was the slowest. Lazy. Pathetic. A joke. He proclaimed, "That's who you are."

She let the lies in.

Nothing he said was helpful. It just hurt.

I pulled the car over so we could look at each other. Looking at someone, offering full attention, is a bridge to healing. I explained how she is wonderfully and beautifully made. I shared unwavering truths that define her. I reminded her that just because someone asks a question does not mean you have to answer. Then I said a bad word. I told her we can't let the idiots stick.

"Idiot" is not a nice word. There are those in life who want to pull you into their pain by pounding you with lies. It takes great courage to be yourself. Long, wish, and strive for achievements. Question. Rest. Meditate. Take in beautiful truths, perhaps hard, but nonetheless beautiful. Don't let the idiots stick.

Consider your power. People become who you tell them they are. So, what do you say? How do you stand? Do you unite or divide? Do you destroy or employ?

Your strength originates from your starting stance.

Do not let others determine how, where, and when you stand.

The courage to be.

Your paramount, unshakable identity is: You are beautiful, loved, and blessed.

The question is: What are you going to do with it?

Live it out in the wonderful, loving, and unique way you are called to do.

Having the courage to be means valuing who you are and how you are wired. You can hail your hallelujahs in the breathtaking and baffling.

We have a neighbor who knows she has early onset dementia. Like many, it is difficult for her to realize she may someday not know her family or home. One night we gathered for a party and I offered to walk her home. We headed out and she stopped, facing in the wrong direction. Her eyes searched the sky. I stood quietly for a moment. She startled me, awaking our silence by calling my name.

"Sarah," she said, "You need to say, 'Hello' to the moon."

"What?" I wondered.

What is a careful question to pose when someone is fading.

I smiled as she looked at me and then gazed at the huge harvest moon. I missed the beauty, focusing on heading home. She knew where she was going. She didn't want to miss a hallelujah.

"I go outside every night and say, 'Hello' to the moon," she explained.

"I know someday I won't remember the moon."

"I want to give thanks while I remember."

She has the courage to be. She is thankful for what she has today. She doesn't want to miss the extraordinary in the ordinary.

Courage is contagious, and its impact lasts long after initiation.

Call and claim your hallelujahs.

Have the courage to be.

You are not the sum of all they see.

Grace looks you in
the eye and longs for
the moment.
Grace is love
in action.

CHAPTER NINE

GRACE

Grace lightens burdens we didn't know we carried.
Grace grabs us by the shoulders,
looks us in the eyes with love,
and says, "It will be okay."

Amazing, abiding, obscure, soft, radical.

Powerful and present.

This is grace.

Grace is a word we often use, a pattern we sometimes see, and sustenance we do not understand. Anne Lamott offers an honest explanation of grace for she admits we cannot fathom its depth, breadth, and life:

> *I do not understand at all the mystery of grace —*
> *only that it meets us where we are but does not*
> *leave us where it finds us.*

Grace is big, beyond us and our individual ability. It is laughter at a painful point when we thought joy moved on to someone else's party. It is the calm in restless nights and in days when we can't believe one more thing has been piled on us. Grace is an elegant, refined movement - a dance with unpredictable changes in acceleration, formation, and aim.

I have a heavy gait and do not tread gracefully, yet no matter the stride – yours or mine, we all walk in grace. With grace, we honor someone by granting its title ("Your Grace") or glorifying their presence, "You graced the world of technology with robust innovation and equality." Like all gifts, we twist its use and intention. Consider the sarcastic utterance coupled with an eye roll for an unwelcomed guest, "Oh yes, he graced us with his presence." Grace is abiding, interceding, and welcoming. It is rest, forgiveness – a do over, a do better. Grace is an identity bringing liberation and connection. Grace is also hard. There is a cost to grace. Sometimes small, sometimes so incalculable it cannot be repaid, and it is okay. It is LOVE.

One February evening, my husband (the fellow known as "Sully") was at a black-tie event, and as he was leaving, he saw an old friend. He walked over to say goodbye and realized his friend was talking with a familiar looking Fortune 100 CEO. When the CEO turned around, they had a nice exchange and Sully noticed a sizeable stain covering his shirt.

Sully quipped, "That looks like the mark of a good party."

The CEO replied, "One of our young associates approached me for a picture and as we were getting in close, he got sick. On me."

This happened on the dance floor. While everyone either immediately froze or scrambled, recognizing the gaff as a career limiting move, the CEO didn't ask for a name or ID badge. He simply asked, "Are you okay?" And then asked others to lend aid.

The cost: brushing aside ego, annoyance, and a dry-cleaning bill.

An unmerited, undeserved action.

Not long ago, Sully was driving our large, old SUV. She is a dark grey mare and we will drive her until she finally collapses, as no one would want her remains. Her stinks and stains are masked by cleaners, fragrances, and mats. She is hearty and durable – perhaps a descriptor we all want at one time or another. Sully had just filled up with gas, run through the car wash, and polished the inside. As he waited at a light to make a right turn, a driver rear-ended him.

An accident is an interruption.

Interruptions are excuses for withholding grace.

Interruptions are precisely where and when grace is needed.

My husband pulled over and found a lanky teenage boy who was apologizing profusely. He could see his lip trembling and tears well up. This kid was heading to a junior year exam. Sully looked at the dent in our right bumper, arguably matching the dent on the left bumper, and looked at the boy. All of it was fixable. He said, "I want you to go from here and do well on your exam, and then I want you to do some nice things for other people. Let this go, but don't let go of kindness."

Sully patted him on the shoulder affirming things would be okay by letting go of the accident. They shook hands, agreed to drive safely, and left.

When we talked about it later, I asked why he was readily calm and not irritated. After all, he was late to a meeting and had just gotten the car cleaned. Sully replied, "I kept thinking about somebody once doing that for me when I was an inexperienced driver. Maybe someone will do it for our kids. No matter if they do or don't, that kid needed grace for the journey."

We all do.

Grace is favor – an extension of time to repay what is owed or a complete pardon. Student loans may offer a six-month grace period after graduation before payments begin. I will never forget the look on a friend's face, when she learned a family member offered to pay off her student loans. Once saddled with ten, fifteen or thirty years of repayment, grace relinquished her burden. Through grace, she could freely begin.

Grace is beautiful and lovely, meek and bold, but defining what is beautiful, lovely, meek, and bold depends on the giver and recipient. Grace can silence hostility, criticism, and rejection. It confounds, comforts, and challenges us.

Grace is gratitude, thanksgiving at the table. Without parameters, dress codes or seating charts, grace simply says, "Come."

Grace is where the trembling stops. It is where the internal chatter shatters into dust leaving glimmers of hope and redemption. Grace reminds us to be careful with life and allows us to fall in love again with our full, whole humanness. Through grace, stories unfold. We see our likeness in each other and a shared knowledge of how little we truly understand. Grace comes in doubt, unease, and emptiness. It comes when you are full, but lack nourishment.

If we seek a whole, thriving, abundant life, then we strive to grow in grace. We give and receive. We recognize and acknowledge it from long ago and today. You cannot live a whole, beautiful life alone. Grace bursts forth in community. It comes even when you don't hear the cry for it in yourself or in others.

Through grace I see my joy complete - not by fixing you, but by accepting myself. Grace illuminates the extraordinary in the everyday.

Grace brings peace. With grit, hope, and love, it binds wounds, allowing scars to form and fade.

Grace teaches us to love life. In grace, we become centered and whole.

But it doesn't stay.

We lose it, not because grace lets go, but because we do.

Grace is a deadline extension, getting precious time with a loved one before they die, or accepting a job offer or declining one before fully knowing if the answer is the right one. It is the breath you take today, tomorrow, and always. It is an act of love. Grace sets the captives free. Grace is the work of the brave.

With grace, you say "hello" and "goodbye." Time and space are honored.

When someone you love is wheeled off to surgery you are forced to let go. Everything is out of your hands. You may only go so far before the surgical team takes over. You wait. You hope and pray. Grace begins its work.

An amazing surgeon, Dr. Joe, repaired our young son Henry's nerve and tendon damage. All the while, another brilliant surgeon healed us. For as we headed to a small private room to wait, we found our dear friend Dr. Allyson. She was not on duty. Henry was not her patient. By grace, we discovered the extraordinary power of presence. She offered a state of grace. She had done the same years before waiting for our youngest Gabrielle to be born. Not her patient. Plenty of others and things to attend to, and yet she came and sat with us and loved.

Grace is love lived out. Our lives transform when friends come, sit, and love. Grace is the gift of being.

Grace is compassion - for with grace, passion comes and says, "You are not alone."

When we brought our son Henry home from the hospital, his big brother Jack would not leave his side. We put them both in our bed. I think an area needing improvement in medical care is the discharge process. The first night at home is hard, no matter if your patient is two days old or eighty-two years old. Everyone is tired. Things do not go as anticipated, and you are rarely fully equipped for all that is needed. The discharge paperwork lacks grace. Nursing moms who had no trouble in the hospital, find the baby won't latch. An elderly patient may experience "sundowning" - a state of confusion and anxiety in the late afternoon and evening. For any age, pain can set in late at night, when medication is not effective, and the pharmacy is out of alternatives or is closed until morning. Worse still, you have a prescription in hand for medication needed to help your asthmatic breath or release pain so your beloved can rest but the pharmacy says insurance will not cover it as written. There is no one to call. It is after hours. There is no money to get the medicine. This is common and unspoken. Where are these warnings and remedies on the discharge papers?

When we finally got Henry home and settled, he had to take medicine around the clock. Being young and in pain, he did not want to take it. We were exhausted and worried. Our heavily bandaged boy lay with tears running down his checks, feeling nauseous and crying, "Mommy, I just can't."

Not knowing what to do, I went to the kitchen thinking I would find something sweet to mix with the medicine. I knew we didn't have ice cream because if we did, I would have eaten it. Weary, I put my hands to my head, praying for his pain to subside. I covered my eyes feeling the weight of my plea. Tired, so tired, the freezer door felt heavy. I pulled open the handle expecting frozen spinach and peas, and to my shock found it was filled with ice cream. Many brands and flavors there for the choosing. Name brands. The good stuff. Not the fifty-gallon vat of Neapolitan Sully gets the kids on vacation and they devour with joy and sprinkles. At the beach, everything and anything tastes good.

This was a holy grail of creamy goodness. I was in awe and tears rolled down my cheeks as I mixed our son's medicine with ice cream and he got it down. Grateful. Awed and humbled by grace. The next day I learned our friend Jeff filled the freezer before we got home. He was so concerned about Henry and decided the situation called for ice cream. He was right beyond measure. It did.

My Uncle Paul had the same philosophy for hard days.

Grace comes in purveyors of ice cream.

Grace is a true companion.

The first night home, Jack stayed with Henry. They both had ice cream. As I left the room to check on their sisters, I could hear Jack whisper, "Henry, I love you. It's okay we both have weaknesses. Yours is glass. Mine is wolves. We'll take care of each other."

With grace, they will.

With grace, we do.

Disgrace. Missed grace.

One winter weekend a group of students were on a school sponsored ski trip. Just off the hotel lobby, adults gathered for a private party with flowing beer, wine, and a punch bowl. Some students joined in. One stayed too long becoming drunk, disruptive, and belligerent. An argument ensued. Things were damaged. Slurs said, likely learned at home and in community, but not addressed. The students and chaperones were asked by management to leave immediately. A long weekend trip abruptly ended after the first night. Buses were loaded and the group headed back to school. Anger, worry, fear, frustration, and exhaustion filled the bus during the ten-hour drive home and later crammed the parking lot where parents waited.

Each parent had a decision to make. How would they greet their child? How would they react if their child snuck beer back to her room or never entered the party? Everyone started leveling out liability. In their first interaction, as the students filed off the bus, would it matter? How do parents love and offer appropriate consequences without condoning bad choices?

Grace allows for an embrace, in lieu of outbursts we later regret. It is not an excuse or coddling, though grace can offer leniency.

I remember hearing the pain of one parent who yelled that day. Repairs take a long time. Initial sutures rupture, requiring added mending. Irritated by other parents, the wait, knowing his daughter drank too much and embarrassed him, he yanked his daughter off the bus, barking obscenities and disappointment. The torrent of punishment lingered for years. This child beat herself up. They both ached, neither knowing how to heal.

The consequences of her poor decisions were ample punishment. No amplification of rage required. She was a good kid who had done something stupid. She knew her father would be angry, and rightfully so, but what she needed coming off the bus was a hug and grace. Restoration could come through hard work to help reimburse costs, sending handwritten apology notes, listening and learning, telling her story, or helping others who did not have the means for ski trips achieve dreams of travel and exploration. Her redemption and renewal for a poor choice would come with service and understanding grace for herself and others. His rage fractured their relationship. Her father spoke of it with heartbroken regret, for at the time he did not know how to accept grace and offer it when it was needed most.

I need grace every time I expose my vulnerabilities and see them as silly and stupid instead of sacred. Grace frees me to release the lies of doubt and shame.

Grace calls you by name.

Grace calls me, calls you, call us by name.

"Worthy." "Beautiful." "Loved."

Grace assures this is who we are.

Grace is the hand taking hold asking you to believe the good, the wonderful, the bountiful dreams unfolding in becoming.

"Worthy," "Beautiful," "Loved," and "Strong" these are your names as you sit exhausted wondering, "Where do I find my people and how will I finally begin to be me?"

Grace stitches your pain with a plan, one small suture at a time. We are lulled into a false sense of learning by grazing over social media feeds. Dive into deeper content and conversations. Clamp on to stories of grace and people who overcome. Believe as you read, "*This is me.*"

Not - will be.

It is me.

Beautifully broken, struggling, hurting, tired and overcoming, even when we are not okay. Grace says right there, right then, "Look, dear child, you are dancing in the divine."

Here we hold these truths: Worthy. Beautiful. Loved. Strong. Possible.

Will you hold them for yourself and others? Prisons are full of missed grace and so is my heart and so are elementary schools where a child may go a whole day without anyone calling her name. To grow in grace, we need to expand our circles. If we come home from meaningful work in faraway places and do not change our influencers and influence, grace is lost - left where it is was found.

There is infinite possibility and places to fully live through grace.

Grace is a random high-five.

Grace is joy rising.

Grace is knowing we are all longing and searching, for grace comes and brings hope during our suffering. Grace is this mystical, daring convergence of hope within our highest pain.

Grace gives you the voice to call out darkness and bring light. With grace, you are life-giving light.

Before exhaustion-fueled irritation has you barking orders or accusations, breathe in grace. Wrap yourself in grace. Swaddle and bind your body so grace sheds the shame. Grace is a warrior's armor and a royal's fragrance. You carry the atoms of both.

Open your arms, cloak others in grace, and the fantastic work of whole living catches fire.

Grace is a voice at the table.

Travel within or far outside the United States, across oceans and rivers, and you find shared stories over memorable meals. Renaissance begins at a table in any locale throughout the world where grit, grace, hope, and love are found.

Begin with grace, for grace is gratitude. More than rote words or pleas, it is a recognition of welcome and gathering. Tables around the world offer respite and recitation of thanks. Shared in a myriad of ways, gratitude comes with warmth billowing from deliciously filled plates, fragrant spices reminding us of childhood comforts, joys in preparing the dish, and smiles from those gathered. We are gracious when pulling up a chair, pouring a glass, and making room when the table seems full. Grace is a toast. Grace is a prayer. Grace is goodness and wholeness.

There is no litmus test, no one is required to reach a threshold to receive a state of grace. Love and grace abide, prevail, flow throughout life whether you are a poet, prophet or prisoner. Sounds great if we are talking about you and me, but what about that guy over there? The one across the street, across the country, across the world. Yes, him.

Or her. What about that gorgeous, size zero over there in the bikini with six kids, a full-time job, backyard chickens and an organic garden, who is always stain-free and arrives on time? Negative self-talk heightens the false perception of perfection. Oh wait, she's bringing you a meal next week. Ugh! The hardship of goodness coming to us in unexpected forms. Grace is available to them. It is available to us when erratic, insecure, mean thoughts arise. This is frustrating in our humanness. It is tough to accept the person opposite you, the innocent one, the one causing pain and poor choices, the one you don't even know, but with whom you disagree politically or dietetically is beautifully, freely able to receive grace. Grace is available for them, for you, and for me. No limits.

Grace swoops in filling gaps of impossibility. Grace is how we go on, like a broken crayon or worn-down oil pastel in an artist's hand beautifully bringing color and meaning. Life is crumbling, broken, and bleak as we cry, "I'm done." Grace comes, bringing rest, renewal, and unexpected openings. Grace calls for astoundingly more. Grace carefully reassembles fractured pieces to create a stained glass window. A blemished, tarnished, lonely, seemingly unusable remnant becomes a catalyst of light. With grace, we discover we can forgive ourselves and others. We fully realize a necessary awesome reliance beyond self.

By grace, we gather.

Gather is a word intersecting work and life. We are a family who gathers at the table. In this communion, we laugh, listen, and talk. We talk a lot. It's wonderful, eye-opening, humbling, messy, and awe-inspiring. If there is frustration, perhaps over what we are eating, a dish I've burned, or a harsh word someone said, we stay. We tell our four kids the most important thing is to love. We talk about worries, thorns, joys, and ways to discover light in darkness. Social technology bombarding our lives makes these talks tough, but also offers vast blessings and resources. Innovation will always endure. We want our kids (Team Sully) to know home is wherever and however we gather.

Gatherings are not always good. Years ago, a wonderful friend said it would not be a vacation with extended family without her spending one night in the bathtub with tears and a large glass of wine. Family is crazy-making, callous, and yet comforting. There are dinners where you would rather pick up venomous snakes by the tail then endure another story or hurl of pain. This is true even for posts of shiny people on the beach in matching white and khaki or large lettered reunion t-shirts. Family knows you and they don't know you. They are part of your story and you are a part of theirs. With grace, you find peace in who you are and all you are becoming. With grace, you see your beautiful uniqueness and individuality. With grace, your whole life is coming alive. Gatherings are easier, not because they change or better wine and food are served, but because you are free in the luscious, curious, captivating wonder of worthiness. Grace takes hold within.

Corporations need to gather. They run into trouble when meals convene after long days of conference lectures. There is little left to bring to the table unless leaders ask questions and get all engaged. These are not questions of interrogation requiring quick replies to demonstrate stellar performance. When done properly, they are initiators for meaningful discussions. Breaking bread, pouring wine, pulling down barriers. It is interesting how often we quickly defend politicians, pundits, and celebrities when we have never taken a seat at their table. Are we as zealous and passionate in celebrating peers?

Hungry people are the best people to serve. Before gathering, make sure attendees are hungry for nourishing life. Adapt when time and exhaustion are hurdles. Get together in the kitchen to make meals, serve others, and sit among them. Sit outside. Provide a relaxed atmosphere, even when significant work is due. Champion the new. Feed new concepts, new people, new means of kinship. Redirect or shut down negative, destructive conversation, but be careful in doing so. Embarrassing or demeaning people can fuel the very thing you want to quash. Amplify grit, grace, hope, and love.

Food and community are vivacious fuel. At your table is where people should come alive.

Remember.

Elmer Isom served on the U.S.S. Utah on December 7, 1941. Elmer was nicknamed "Blackie." He was a Seaman Third Class who survived the bombing of Pearl Harbor. He never returned for reunions. He did not like to talk about the day a sleepy port, the paradise of the Hawaiian Territory, became hallowed ground. He was below deck when the attack began. Explosions alerted senior officers to command, "To general quarters!"

All followed orders and manned their battle stations. Blackie raced up to the deck to see an explosion decapitate his chief. Eventually, he and other crewman jumped off the ship and swam through fire, screams, bullets, and blood until they reached the shore. During the latter years of his life, when Alzheimer's robbed his memory of friends and family, Blackie recalled serving on the U.S.S. Utah and painted pictures of the ship. The U.S.S. Utah still rests in the harbor waters. It is called the Forgotten Memorial.

Across the island, Admiral Isaac Campbell Kidd, Sr., was likely on the bridge of the U.S.S. Arizona, on the morning of December 7, 1941. Usually known as "Cap" to family and friends, Admiral Kidd was Commander of Battleship Division ONE and a Rear Admiral. His leadership was legendary because of the relationships he forged. He routinely walked the length of battleship row, engaging with seaman and officers. He made it a point to personally know every man on his ship. Long before cell phones or reminder apps, he taped detailed notes about his shipmates, their wives and families, to his bathroom mirror and reviewed the notes as he shaved in the morning. He sought personal relationships and connections.

On this bright Sunday morning while some were still asleep, Japanese fighter planes dropped bombs down the smokestacks of the U.S.S. Arizona causing the ship to explode and list. Admiral Kidd was last seen manning the guns trying to shoot down enemy planes. His body was never found. Days later, salvage divers recovered his sea chest, the Naval ring that had earlier been on his finger, and his binoculars. Inside the chest were his Naval uniforms, sword, engraved knife, plumed hat, and love letters from his wife, Inez. The U.S.S. Arizona is recognized now as a sacred tomb and an active ship. Soldiers must salute as they sail by. Admiral Kidd is to this day considered missing in action. He received the Congressional Medal of Honor and the Purple Heart medal, posthumously. There are three battleships named after him.

Few officers' wives or dependents were allowed on Pearl Harbor before the attack. Second Lieutenant Paul Coursey and his wife Mary had a baby boy named John. Lt. Coursey's room was near Admiral Kidd's quarters. Mary wanted to go to Pearl Harbor and hoped Admiral Kidd's wife would join her, but she declined as her son Isaac Campbell Kidd, Jr., would soon be coming home for Christmas break from the Naval Academy.

Mary and John lived ten miles from Pearl Harbor. On Saturday, December 6, a friend and fellow officer had a date and asked Lt. Coursey to switch shifts. Lt. Coursey agreed and this decision saved his life. He was home with Mary and John when the bombing began. A doctor nearby owned a car and he rushed Lt. Coursey to his ship.

He headed to the U.S.S. Arizona dock and found apoplectic chaos. Planes flew overhead launching bombs and rapidly firing bullets. Bodies were in the water. Some swimming to shore, some lost in the sea. Lt. Coursey could have headed back to Mary and John. Instead, he bravely jumped in a boat to reach his ship and fight a harrowing battle. Pushing through sirens, screams, and confusion, dodging bullets with his sight on the battered battleship, another bomb hit, downing the bow, snapping lines and sinking the U.S.S. Arizona. Lt. Coursey survived, but Mary would wait for weeks to hear if he lived, had been injured, or where he was stationed.

A salvage and recovery crew retrieved Lt. Coursey's pen set, commission papers, Marine saber, and two ashtrays. His dress whites were discovered too, but they solemnly remain. Today, they rest just beyond his open cabin door, hanging in the submerged U.S.S. Arizona. A tomb and an active ship carries warriors and a pressed uniform, remembering noble soldiers who valiantly serve and defend.

Admiral Kidd, Jr., "Ike," was a Naval Academy cadet when his father died. Even though he attained a perfect score on his entrance exam, he wanted to be a train engineer, not a Naval officer. Pearl Harbor changed his course. The United States was now at war and the Navy quickly called cadets to serve. The Academy graduated midshipmen early on December 19, 1941. Admiral Kidd, Jr., never liked to talk about what happened to his father. He could not bring himself to open the letters written by his mom and dad. From his father he learned a lesson he later taught his own kids – "You never wear the stars." You serve, lead, and do not brag or condescend. He was knighted by the Queen of England and served as Commander in Chief and Supreme Allied Commander of the Atlantic Fleet.

He had six children, one of whom is Mary. For years, she has bravely manned her own ship. Mary is the center force of grace at a public elementary school. She knows each family by name. Whether arriving with joys or coming in tentatively with pain, she thoughtfully attends, inspiring courage. Her message: You can. End of story. Her addition: I'm here. And she is, every day. I know this because she greeted my children; she greets them still. I have watched her weep and hug families when a parent has passed or a child is injured. I've seen her high-five or rise and run around her desk to throw her arms around someone who no one else knew needed a hug. She breathes beautiful relationships.

Japanese Admiral Isoroku Yamamoto oversaw the attack on Pearl Harbor. His son also rose to the rank of Admiral. Through grace, two sons of war shared a meal in 1978. Mary remembers her father inviting Admiral Yamamoto to their home. Despite personal pain and a nation still healing, with grace her father offered an enemy a seat at the table.

Blackie Isom had a family of five girls. He served in the kitchen on Navy ships and enjoyed being in the kitchen at home. I knew him. He was kind to me. He made the groom's cake at our wedding. He lovingly helped raise my husband as a doting and dutiful grandfather. His valiant swim, survival, and grace were precursors to my joy.

Lt. Coursey and Mary's family grew with two more children and five granddaughters. Their granddaughter Amy is a brilliant designer. When rain destroyed a ceiling and furniture in my house, she arrived with love and said, "We've got this."

Already under stress from other demands, she assured we would easily mend. She thoughtfully asked about my favorite color – green and noticed there was little of it in our collection of disparate pieces. She restored my strength and renewed a room, bringing jewel tones and joy. Every day our family is thankful for her graciously giving us a place to gather. Amy is a woman who charges ahead when bullets fly. She is a person to call for courage, grace, and talking through the right thing to do even when it is hard to do the right thing. She pulls survivors from tough waters.

Blackie, Paul, Cap, Ike, Mary, Amy, and me. All of these lives, imperfect, brave, fragile, lovely, and broken, weave together through a tapestry of grace.

You and I are here today because of grace. Grace has nothing to do with balance. It is not about our perception of equal distribution. Grit, grace, hope, and love exist, ebb, and flow. Changes in temperature, pressure, and capacity may change us, but with each variation and iteration we can chose to grow in grit, grace, hope, and love. They move us from deficient and incomplete to wholeness and satisfaction. They ignite freedom to stop, change course, or pursue multiple passions – regardless if the world thinks these pursuits are doable, advisable, or linked.

They may not immediately remove pain but will empower us to push through when facing weapons of destruction.

You have a tapestry of kinship – ties and bonds with people related to you not by blood, but by grace. What do you want to do with this gift? What do you need to do? Unfold the touch points by sharing your stories.

What are you afraid of doing?

What do you dream to do?

Grace means it is okay to rest, have fun, and bring back joy. Grace offers time – an hour, a day, an undetermined interim – to walk without making fist clinched decisions or deriving immediate solutions.

Grace calls, "Remember." Recall the bravery, sacrifice, and choices shaping all you become. Remember the good you can do, the good here now, and the good to come. Bear in mind the wounds of words and weapons. Remember to prevent malice from persisting. Remember the slithering, subtle work of darkness as you wrestle with fear and moral responsibility.

Long forgotten are the pearl pins worn by women to remember the attack on Pearl Harbor.

Long forgotten are the small, daily struggles where grace intercedes.

Fuzziness of memory can confuse what we recall.

What do you pin on your heart and head to remind you of grace and goodness?

Remember the pearls of grace.

CHAPTER TEN

BELIEVE

What advice would you whisper to your younger self? Would you comprehend the radical joys, trembling, and growth to come?

If I could give my younger self advice in one word it would be: Believe.

Back then and today, this wisdom is sound, and not enough.

Acclaimed actress Helen Mirren was asked this question and gave a salty reply, "I'd tell more people to f*** off."

What did you need to hear yesterday or twenty years ago?

Maybe younger is fifteen years, five years or five minutes ago.

What shall I say?

What advice sticks at seventeen and seventy?

Here's a start.

Dear Sarah,

Hold on to faith. Trust God. Stay curious for what you do not fully understand. As a parent tenderly holds a child, cradle in holiness and mercy.

Believe in yourself. You are loved. You are enough. You are called to carry.

Believe in greatness far beyond yourself.

At whatever stage you are, there is a secret, radiant gift to discover. It is the joy in becoming. Life is filled with surprises, clutter, and uncertainty combining with wild and wondrous delights, triumphs, and love. It is the process of becoming - the awkward, startling, and exquisite molding of your whole life.

Do not miss the marvels in being and becoming. Advocate. Love mercy, walk humbly, seek justice, restore relationships, offer compassion, and embrace the sanctuary of silly, goofy, and home.

With friends:

Relationships give life meaning. Fuel yourself with soulful friendships. Great relationships are conscious fellowship.

A friend is one who will gently yank a stray hair from your chin, mid-story and keep going. Stray hairs appear after having children and no one warns you of this or leaky boobs and bladders or how you change in relationships. Even if they did, you may not listen or understand. Love where you are, as you are - errant hairs and all.

If you are constantly looking for approval, you aren't free to beautifully, boldly become. Don't let someone else be the arbiter of your dreams. Don't abdicate the throne of your life. This world needs you. Act on it.

Let loose. Daydreaming, whimsy, and creative arts change the world.

Have the important conversations and work on perfecting the art of love. Savor those life-filling talks; journal the inspiration and effect.

If you are vulnerable and someone later wounds you by breaking your trust, work through the pain and forgive them. It is not an immediate pardon. This violation will knock down your confidence. Letting go of resentment, hate, and hope for revenge is an onerous art. Forgiveness does not deny the pain. It is the resilient work of renewal in you. In time, you will find there are other resplendent souls to help you heal. They are people who will hold your vulnerability as a treasured gift. Guard your heart, acknowledge the relationship has changed, and give thanks for knowing who you are and who they are. Cut away from cruelty. Don't draw from wells of disdain. Allow these awful experiences to fortify your heart, enlighten who you can trust, and marvelously shape the ways you love yourself and others.

You will meet new friends throughout life who will love you just as if you were inseparable since preschool. Love each other through changes. Keep your core of folks who feel like home. Welcome more. Some people are closer for seasons. Others come in and out of our lives because of time, distance, and choices. Love them all.

Sarcasm and greetings that begin with a cut-down are cancerous.

Listen to how people introduce you. Be mindful of how you introduce others. Build each other up. If someone introduces you by sharing how you were puny and hurting and they rescued you, they do not honor you. Run with those who honor.

Be around good people who do not look like you. Learn from them.

With family:

Lead a life you will look back on with love. Dwell in optimism, eagerness, and bliss.

It's an astounding thing to begin your day by hearing, "I love you. I missed you while you were sleeping." Never take for granted that the people you love know how you feel. Make the most of "hellos," "goodbyes," and the vast in between.

Upcoming vacations are exciting. Renovations are maddening. Don't let the big finish get in the way of enjoying the creation. Relish in the every-

day happiness of being together, even if togetherness is a quick meal, folding laundry, picking paint colors, an in-depth talk before bed, or simply sharing funny quips on a group text.

You, your parents — all of us - are imperfect people. Love heals a multitude of poor choices.

Family members may inadvertently or intentionally label. Behaviors from age 13 adhere at age 35. Expectations can rest in false narratives and negative, fuzzy memories. Be careful in pigeon-holing people as who they are today for what they did growing up. Work to know each other as adults through fresh eyes and shared grace.

If ever you feel like you can't be yourself amongst extended family or in a group, shine on and move on. Be you. No explanation needed. Weird is where wonder grows.

"Calm down!" - "Chill out!" - "Relax!" are unfulfilled commands. Try a loving whisper rather than a shout to get to the crux of the concern.

Take care of each other. One day a hurt will come and throttle you, perhaps because of heartache from long ago resurfacing at an inconvenient time. When pain knocks you down, getting the right help is a sign of strength. Trust each day, regardless of little ups and downs. Believe everything will eventually be okay. With laughter, humility, compassion, rest, faith, grit, grace, hope, and love, it will.

Family is defined by love and is found when you are completely at home. Love is where giving and receiving are not a sacrifice; they are sacred gifts.

You will find the love of your life when you know he is your best friend, when you bring out the best in each other, and when at your worst, he is all in and you are too. You'll know he is the one because your joy comes by bringing each other joy. Ask yourselves difficult questions before walking down the aisle. Seek counseling, even during moments of bliss. It will make issues, such as loading the dishwasher, finances or "Where will we spend next Christmas?" or "Who ate all the ice cream?" a lot easier.

Some of the greatest gifts come in winks rather than a symphony of fireworks.

At work:

Lead in love. Put love in action. Wondering how? Consider the most loving thing to do. People will long remember the ways you love. Pour love on the ones you like the least. Grit, grace, hope, and love are never wasted.

The person or people who intimidate you are just as insecure as you are. Everybody has bouts of doubt and diarrhea. Gross, certainly. Life, actually. Those folks appearing more fit, savvy, and coiffed are no more valuable, and no less.

Work hard – paid or volunteer. Offer to work the midnight shift and holidays.

No one - except the facilitator - likes when a meeting begins with, "Let's go around the room and tell something about ourselves." Flop sweat starts here.

Pursue things that are not seemingly sensible. Earn a double major in business and theater. Minor in bagpiping and bakery science. Be an entrepreneur and attorney. Be lots of things, including non-traditional. None of it has to gel with others.

No one ever became a Fortune 100 CEO and said it was all due to the 16 Advanced Placement® classes she took in high school. Stop rushing everything. Take the pottery class in lieu of Latin V. It may help mold future decisions.

Popularity is not the goal. A grand, robust whole life stems from your thoughtful impact on others.

"30 under 30," "40 under 40," are lists. They are not identities. You are beloved and wonderfully made. This is your identity - no qualifiers, social media campaigns or fundraisers required.

A lonely, restless spirit is one who can masterfully create or break. Consider your influences.

Getting outside, taking a long hot bath, and singing loudly in the car are highly underrated rejuvenation.

A few of your favorite bosses, family members, and friends will lead lives treading slowly on a revolving loop of poor choices. Stay out of the loop. Love them anyway.

Every relationship will have some off days. Let go of trying to change them. Focus on who you want to be.

Find ways to cheer people on - or up - before complaining. Negativity, hate, and mocking are weapons of mass destruction. Listen, offer solutions, bring people together.

Feedback is fine, but praise, boos or mehs shouldn't rattle your soul. Adapt and adjust as needed.

A time will come when a man or a woman will look at you and you will feel uncomfortable. Stand up for yourself. Protect your body and spirit. Stay or walk away with power and resolve. Never be ashamed. Stand up for others.

Feel good about what you are wearing when you enter a party. Underdressed or overdressed, go with confidence. Your laughter, presence, and engagement are what people see, want, and remember. Don't assume every other attendee has it all together; they don't, nor do you. Your arrival, your career, your accomplishments, and goals are your own. Run your race and stop stressing to catch up. You might be chasing a life that doesn't exist.

Inexperience isn't an obstruction; see it as invigorating.

Get visible in your work or industry. Become a go-to expert in certain areas or in one small slice. Do this when no expects it, meaning do it because you chose to, not because someone asked you.

Dreams take help and time to form, shape, and actualize. Overnight success and achieving greatness alone are illusions. Life is thankfully never a one man show.

Falling down is a gift. It is where life's great stories originate.

We each are an integral part of a great masterpiece. Every role matters.

In life:

You are alive; today is a splendid time for a new beginning. Go!

You are able. You are more equipped than you realize for this present circumstance. Aid abounds. Stop worrying. Stop lying in bed wresting over the little thing you said or did. Pray more. Be with people who invigorate your spirit. Love your rambunctious self.

Be a person of confident "Yes," "No," "Maybe" and "I don't know." Own what you create – joy, art, mess, magic.

Decide in advance who you are. Know who you are on Monday morning, so you are ready for what comes on Saturday night.

Every life is worthy of love. Serve. Help people. Welcome strangers. Do what awakens your soul. Awaken others to their dreams. And laugh. Deep belly laughs are everything. Don't go long without them.

Be kind. This is not easy. It is a warrior's work. You'll mess this up and others will too. Try again. It will still provide for great stories around the dinner table.

Yes, that was a rotten thing he did. Yes, she is nuts. These real experiences make fabulous fiction. Write. Share your stories. Change names as needed. Find the funny. Move on.

Express gratitude. Acknowledge beauty. Speak truth with love. Do not be daunted by compounding pain in this world. You are a magnificent, wounded healer.

Don't marginalize pain. Life is tinged with shadows. Dig deeper into why and where you hurt. While sinking too long in self-pity causes harm, acknowledging a loss is a powerful release. Pay attention to sorrow and fatigue. Are you walking with grief or in grief? Is there an exhaustive worry taking up too much room in your heart and head? Toss it, paint it, write a story, or talk with a friend. Brave warriors get outside help for inside battles.

An excited utterance is often a prayer.

Exhaustion, a tiredness in your marrow, is commonly missed before it wallops and wounds. Fatigue is when we start to lose things like keys and tempers. Plan ahead to simplify your life as best you can when stress is high. Routines for bolstering body, mind, and spirit will become great allies.

Take advantage of readily available cures. Sleep renews and awakens us.

Sometimes the life you are living is hard, and it is right where you are needed. Easy and fair are tenuous. Don't give up when things get rough. The majority will quit, while you are just getting started.

If you love church, dancing, and dinners with friends, go. If they are causing pain, assess where you are. Find communities that make you better in love, work, and life. Occasionally the least loving people stand in pulpits or wear diamond crosses and badges of faith. Look for those who love and carry others without ego, gossip, or self-centered agenda. Some are disguised as talented songwriters in Nashville bars.

Consider your actions, presence, and impact in a room and online, even if you think no one is watching.

The ideal apology is a change of behavior.

Unexpected, authentic encouragement is a matchless gift for every soul. Text the CEO or shower the sales clerk with simple, sincere inspiration for what lies ahead.

Take risks. Give yourself grace. Know everything does not have to happen now. Oprah and your law school professor were right, "You can have it all. Just not all at once." But you don't need it all right now.

You are designed for delicious, divine more – more hard stuff than you can imagine and more love than you can hold. Grow in the more. In the thick of the yuck is where we find glory – our seemingly impossible – and our people.

Odds and Ends:

"What's that smell?" This is a question without a satisfactory answer.

Avoid unnecessary qualifiers: "We need to talk." "Don't get mad at this…" "To be honest…"

Seek wise counsel. Trust your gut. Build friendships of varied ages, stages, and backgrounds.

When people yell, they often aren't articulating the real pain.

Grant grace and receive it. You see more miracles with grace.

Conflict is not inherently bad. Debate and differing opinions are needed for growth if they are offered with respect.

Sunday night stress is a common curse. Rituals aid in lessening the lament. Rejuvenate. Don't decimate.

Exercise. Enjoy the meal, a glass of goodness, and great people. Eat the cake. Moderation makes for better parties and triathlon partners. "Opera-

tion Hot Body 20XX" starts, pauses, and recommences at any time of your choosing. No matter the flaws and globs you see, love who you are right now.

Go to events, often. Stay home and snuggle, often. Make it a point to wrap your arms around all in your home and tell them you love them, often.

Very few of us are morning people. Greet the day, your roommates, spouse, and kids with warmth before the coffee brews.

People are honored when we remember the wonderful, hard, and holy. Tell people of the great impact in their small deeds. Write notes and texts with specific joys, thanks, and loves. Share the words you need to hear. When someone texts, "You are phenomenal – a superbly kind-hearted friend," reply with more than a mere, "Thank you" or smiling emoji. They see you. See them.

When life is draining, and you are not yourself, find the resolve to claim, "Enough!" Let "plucky" be an apt descriptor of your tenacious spirit. All you need for your whole life is in your grasp. Let go of what harms and hinders.

Recognize when you are standing on holy ground – places of awe and restoration.

Be mindful of what you activate and amplify.

There is nothing wrong with staying away from toxic people or banana heads or both. Do it, as needed.

Invite people over and don't apologize for the state of your home. In fact, just quit apologizing so much, in general.

If you are wondering if you should shower, go ahead and shower.

It feels great to stand for something and someone, even if you are a bit wonky or wobbly in the moment. Speak out if things are ever disturbingly odd or frighteningly familiar.

Be careful before choosing permanent reminders of temporary feelings. Every decision has consequences. Consider what you want your life to look like and work backwards.

If you are scared, forge ahead in the fear. Talk to it. Claim it and take away its power.

The one in front of the camera doesn't necessarily have the wisdom or the power. Not every adult is smart. Not every teacher offers great advice. The youngest person in the room may be the wisest.

Logic is not always a reliable anchor. It's okay to feel your way through a struggle without recognizing an immediate solution.

Save more money than you think you might need. When you travel abroad and find art you love in budget, buy it.

Capture moments, and not just with pictures. Be in the moment.

Talk to yourself like a best friend, not an enemy or insecure co-worker.

Every comment does not require a reply. Every drama does not require your immediate action. People will long remember kindness or rudeness that is beyond what is anticipated.

You will become the person you decide to be.

It is okay to wait. Good ideas and great love need courage and time. Passions are tough to pin down. Do not worry. Press on in service and joy. You find meaning in serving and doing good works. Trust there is goodness even in the difficult and ugly. You can always learn something — maybe how to run faster and sooner.

Marriages last when people love even when they don't feel like loving. Get help and advice if you and Sully are ever failing to bring out the best in each other. It happens in small steps. Lots of French fries seem like a good idea, so do sweater vests. Neither help the other.

Making babies when you want them and are ready for them is spectacular. Intimacy forms in divine ways on holy ground throughout your whole life, often with your clothes on. Protect your sacred spaces.

Motherhood is astounding, awesome, tough, radical, quiet, and transforming. Quiet comes in hugs and watching wonder. Children discover their hands, a sound, an ability to do cartwheels, and create. You are honored to be a part of their becoming. You are vital to their becoming. Read. Seek expertise. Read to become a better person and parent. Read more to raise good people. Let them see you read and hear you read so they will read. Despite every best intention at some point you will absentmindedly reply, "Fine. Whatever." Remember, the ensuing mess is partly one of your making. Admire it. Make them clean it up.

Your worry and ache for your children will surpass any self-related pain on your heart. This is an intricate part of parenthood. Be the adult you want your children to become. Choose harder parenting. Decide if you want to raise obedient rule followers or self-reliant decision-makers. Raising wise decision-makers is the harder parenting with the greater reward.

As you get older, you will have to exercise more, eat less of the things you love and yet your body will still not cooperate. You head to the pool and see white bikinis on fifty-year-olds who look better than you did at thirty-five. Let's just admit that even at fifteen a white bikini on you would have appeared as an embarrassing see-through experience when wet. Wear what makes you feel good. If it's board shorts and rash guard shirts, surf on. Women's bathing suits are ridiculous and rarely functional for more than accidentally revealing bodily pieces and parts you want covered. You love the water; go swim.

Sully is the love of your life. Grow with him. Get fit with him – spiritually, physically, and emotionally. Go on dates. In the chaos of grabbing water bottles, making lunches, and heading out the door, stop for a kiss. Let your kids see your love.

Speak of joys, sorrows, and loss. Go to weddings and funerals. Mourn with those who mourn. Rejoice with those who lovingly rejoice. Honor births, deaths, and moments when you feel the nudge of love. Comfort those who are struggling. You have enormous capacity to bring heaven on earth in your still, quiet presence.

Surprise people with joy. Be the joy. Find the joy. It is there, and so easily missed.

Put down the phone. Look in the eyes of someone who loves you. The way to joy for your whole life is to give away all the good you gather. You will end up with more.

Interruptions are opportunities for grit, grace, hope, and love. Build bridges of restoration.

Hold fast to your source of strength. Choose LOVE above all else.

Carry and wield it well.

This advice is far from complete. Couple this with what you know to be true. Fruit on pizza is gross. Mayonnaise and sunlight are never a good combination. And despite persistent evidence to the contrary, life is beautiful, wonderful, and good.

Be the beautiful, wonderful, and good.

With love,

Sarah

And with that, I'm armed and anchored.

No, it doesn't cover every imaginable scenario and more could be said, but you and I are ready for mountains, valleys, and deserts and the surly and exciting beasts within.

And so, I ask you to consider:

What advice would you give your younger self?

Write a letter.

Wondering how to begin?

Here is a start.

> *Dear Younger Self,*
>
> *You are so loved.*
>
> *You are enough.*
>
> *Go. Love others.*
>
> *Love,*
>
> *Me*

CHAPTER ELEVEN

BECOMING

Rejoice in fragility.
Find your joy of living.

Sully and I met in a high school biology class. My friend Shannon waved me over to sit next to her and said, "Save a seat for Chris Sullivan. He's so funny." We did. He was. We later learned we had been on the same tennis team at the ages of twelve and thirteen. We vaguely remembered each other. I knew at seventeen I would marry this boy. He knew he would marry me. I did not tell anyone, neither did he. By twenty-one we were engaged and soon married. We waited eight years to have kids. I treasure our time to become. I think in many ways it sustained us. For we grew together, learning how to love, fight, and share intimacy in ways beyond sex. Like when you rush home from work and are violently ill with food poisoning. Or when you are hurting, cut deeply by family, a co-worker or a friend and your spouse stands by, not to fix, but to listen and comfort. Learning to listen takes time. It's hard to listen with little ones underfoot as cries, exhaustion, feedings, and milestones interrupt, or rather, erupt. The easier route is to snap out a solution.

We fell in love with each other's beautifully broken souls. We just didn't know we were broken. Few of us do. How great it would be if we could all rejoice in our fragility. We were young - our barely twenties frontal lobes still developing. We were smart, naïve, hard-working, passionately pursuing dreams, and inside, scared. Fortunately, we found community with others wanting to grow strong in marriage and life. Early on we learned the best advice: When you don't feel loving, if there is disconnect, love anyway.

A prosperous marriage, family, and life require finding joy and giving thanks in the glorious as well as the ho-hum. It is a heavy order when you move from wanting to tear each other's clothes off every hour to dealing with bills and struggles of doubt and fear disguised as anger, irritation or indifference. When tectonic plates collide, the crust crumples and pushes upwards to form mountains. When people collide, they have fun, make babies, and sometimes destroy each other. The destruction may not come from harsh words, but rather ignoring and neglecting.

Nobody wants to hear about their parents' sex life. Over the years we heard my dad was a minister known for providing pre-marital counseling where he encouraged couples to "be faithful to each other in marriage and have sex all the time. It is wonderful with the person you love and just gets better and better."

Two words: Hooray and Ewwwww!

This is the same fella who said I could not have a Barbie® pool house because Ken and Barbie's marital status and commitment were unclear. I miss my dad. He had the ability to offer so much joy and encouragement that if you approached him for advice on running for public office, you'd leave knowing you should run and he'd readily aid in the campaign. Before you were out the door, he would likely start making calls on your behalf. No matter your faith, political or economic preferences, my dad loved everybody. His heart rested in working on behalf of hurting people. Those in poverty, jail, facing economic and social injustice, and the lost and lonely had a champion in my dad.

People found themselves serving, opening their homes, and softening their hearts because of his encouragement. He was relentless when he saw a need. Imagine sitting at your dinner table and your pastor, Ken Crossman, calls to say he's bringing a homeless person over. They'd both stay for dinner.

My dad had no concept of time. Mom remembers when they lived within walking distance of the church and she could hear the bells ringing for a wedding and him whistling in the shower. Somehow, he made it and got things done.

As a friend shared:

Joie de vivre!

"This familiar French phrase describes him well. There is about him, even to those like myself who have known him only briefly, a bubbling quality of happy excitement which clearly communicates that he has been caught up utterly in a kind of special 'joy of living.' He radiates charm, good will, and a full and deep satisfaction that he is permitted to be alive in a world like ours. Being around him is a tonic for the depressed and disillusioned."

Dad held an unabashed love for human beings and confidence in their potential. Our youngest, Gabrielle Joy, is named for him. She wanders off and we all begin looking for joy. Her presence is joy found. When she was three years old, Gabrielle loved seeing our friends, Jeff and Nanette. Mainly, it was Jeff she wanted to see while his wife Nanette was the lady interloper. One August day Gabrielle raced across a room to hug him and hold his hand. Feeling so much joy and happiness, she did what you do when you grasp something wonderful and have no words – she licked his hand.

I didn't know what to say. Jeff gave the perfect reply. He didn't let go.

Like Gabrielle, sometimes people did not know how to handle Dad's infectious joy.

Perfect? Hardly. Dad had no understanding of how to operate anything technical and hastily pulled the plug to turn something off. He was hearty with a jolly belly laugh, coupled with a handle bar moustache and pocket watch arguably making him resemble an old-time boxer, Santa Claus, or a distant kin to Freddy Mercury, the late lead singer of Queen. For years my mom had a sign in their bathroom:

"Kissing a man without a moustache is like eating an egg without salt."

This adage hung above literature piled in a basket. Always avid readers, there was not a corner in our home you could venture into without finding a good book. I should ask Mom if she picked out this quote or if he did. Either way, it confused me but made me smile as a child.

It's funny how things are comforting even when we don't fully understand.

His work was hard and of his choosing. At times, it nearly broke him – for when leaders realize you are good at bringing people out of crisis, you tend to get thrown into a lot of chaos. If you are not careful and cognizant, your strengths can become burdens, both spiritually and financially. Your gifts build you or break you.

While Dad was in graduate school at Emory University, obtaining a master's in theology and becoming a pastor, he served small churches in North Georgia. He was a student country preacher. It was the 1960s, times abounding with racial turmoil, injustice, and economic frustration. The area Mom and Dad served was known as "Carjacking Country" and it was not unusual to see cars chained to trees and fence posts. But, some of the church folks were carjackers as well. Since my parents were on a four-party phone line (common back then), my dad asked to have a private line installed as he occasionally heard confessions and provided counseling. Church leaders turned him down for what they thought was a sound reason – nobody else had a private line.

Where Mom and Dad did not want privacy was in their outspoken work for equality. A racist by his own admission, ax wielding Lester Maddox was running for governor. Mom and Dad voted in the church building. Everyone knew how they voted. When the weekly paper came out, they recorded the church count – 87 votes for Maddox; 2 for Other.

Early on, Dad attended services with Martin Luther King, Sr., and later stood with giants of the Civil Rights movement. So much of what he and Mom accomplished was heeding a call stirring inside and then going, assured only that they were cloaked in love. People can spend a life time thinking, waiting, but never doing.

Comments once shouted from front porches and bellowed behind closed doors with indignant ignorance or unabashed hate are now hollered on social media. We watch. But do we intercede and serve? Do we act beyond a click or swipe? The small idea pounding on your heart or nudging your shoulder beautifully becomes because of you. Masterful movements throughout generations begin with ordinary people standing in extraordinary light - the luminous rouses the seemingly lowly. First steps are full of risks, but if you never show up, serve the meal, or gather a few together, who will? Go. Love.

Dad stood up against the Ku Klux Klan in their homes and neighborhoods. He founded urban ministries to bring people together, regardless of race or economic backgrounds. Mom and Dad taught young people how to build better relationships by no longer fearing skin color. They loved, learned, and led all while becoming.

Our son Jack, like his grandfather, is an outstanding orator and has a passion for history and helping people become. He shares Sully's wonderful sense of humor and height. Jack recently noted his grandfather was a slimmer William Howard Taft, a descriptor Dad would not have enjoyed, but the pocket watch, handle bar moustache, and robust life attest otherwise.

William Howard Taft was the only U.S. President to serve as Chief Justice of the Supreme Court. He administered the oath of office to two other presidents. I wonder if he did so with whispered warnings, for Taft is credited with describing the White House as "the loneliest place in the world." He found his highest calling as a Supreme Court Justice and feigned having no memory of serving as president.

William Howard Taft had the most powerful position in the world and when his tenure ended, he was still becoming. He could have settled down on a dairy farm or sat behind an ornate desk in a prestigious law firm with little to do, but he became more.

We can too.

Look out for the other guy.

Dad carried quarters, cough drops, calling cards, and handkerchiefs in every suit and pants pocket he owned. Quarters were helpful in the era of pay phones, for if you had quarters in your pocket you were not deemed helpless. Quarters meant you had someone to call. Quarters coupled with calling cards meant people could call Dad. A handkerchief felt better on his nose, and therefore assuredly gave comfort to anyone else sneezing or suffering. He'd give you a clean one and would not ask for it back.

I carry on this handy hankie tradition. There is something reverent, beautiful, and bonding in sharing a keepsake for tears. Hold it and you know you are not alone. Carry something with you each day that you can readily give away. A healthy snack, mints, water, tissues, your undivided attention - are compassion's kindred spirits.

He was an ardent collector and giver, which is difficult on your family when you don't have much money. Dad carried a great deal on his heart and in his hands. When he was young, he traveled to England as a top salesman for Yardley of London. There, he fell in love - with an Austin Healey. He loved the car so much he shipped it home but carried the grill on the plane. Mom had two babies before I arrived, and the sleek British convertible didn't make sense with a growing family and a new career as a pastor. He sold it, but never forgot it.

Years later, I arrived and very soon thereafter a baby brother. In many more, I married Sully and we began our own family. Dad retired and a year later suffered an allergic reaction from two antibiotics leading to renal failure. He went on dialysis for nine years. A new becoming arose. Mom and Dad became advocates for national kidney foundations while still serving others. Eventually, Dad's body weakened. He went into the hospital for a final stay. I hopped on a plane arriving in his hospital room in the early morning hours. Quiet and dark, I slowly opened the door and there he was waiting for me. He knew he was dying and yet still wonderfully becoming.

My heart swelled, I could feel tears coming as I gave him a big smile. He said,

"Sarah girl, you opened the door and light filled the room. Come here."

He knew how to welcome.

We hugged. Cried. We held hands. We have the same hands and eyes.

For my whole life Dad provided "the nook." This was the perfect spot on either side, near his collar bone where I could rest my head as he held me. In that nook, all was well, no matter what bombarded my heart and head. Flopping next to him on a couch to watch television or telling him something scary, worrisome or funny, the nook was a place of grace.

We continue this tradition in our own family. Little Sullys have spaces of love and becoming.

We all need spaces of love and becoming.

We need nooks.

A wonderful friend has an ample bosom. It is a sacred space - not for the reasons you think, potty mind. I went to a funeral just a few weeks after my dad died. It was too soon. As the service closed, I headed out the back door wanting to avoid seeing anybody. I knew I'd burst into tears. Pushing open the huge white door, I was greeted by blinding sunlight and my friend's open arms. Somehow, she had rushed out ahead to flank me and love me.

Even as Dad was heading to hospice, he sat up in his hospital bed, stretched out his arm, and readied the nook.

He said, "Today, we are going to talk about hospice and going home." I had come to care for him, and he commenced the conversation.

He went on, "It's an amazing thing the kind of care you get. Did you meet the nurses yet?"

The introductions began. They attended to him. The family would soon convene with his doctors and he would go home for hospice care. The hospital had a valet service and as we wheeled Dad out the hospital door, he seemed comfortable and at ease. I whispered to the young attendants, "Please don't make him wait on the car. This is his last ride home." They obliged.

I left Sully with our two boys so I could move in with Mom and Dad for this long goodbye. The doctors thought the duration could be a few days or perhaps weeks. It was our son Henry's first birthday. Sully said, "Go."

Dad and I had long talks, laughter, a few songs, and lots of "I love yous." Not enough. There could never be enough. I am thankful for what we had.

Family came. Food filled the kitchen. In those first few days, Dad laughed and engaged while we sat at the table.

Sleep came for longer periods as his body grew weaker and could not expel the toxins.

Sully came to say goodbye to his hero. He loved my dad, a man who shaped him and helped him beautifully become. He called me shortly before he arrived and said, "Honey, help your Dad up so he can look out the window."

Dad had not been outside since we arrived home. He carefully sat up and slowly walked over to the window. There was Sully waving from a convertible. He hollered, "Come out and let's go for a ride."

Sully knew my dad would love one more drive with the top down, feeling the wind in his hair. He handed him driving gloves, and they both laughed as Chris drove and Mom and I rode in the backseat. We waved at people and Dad let out a "Weeeee-hoooo!"

One of the best days in one of the worst times.

Nurses came to bathe him, and Mom lovingly let me stay. We attended. We prepared him. This wasn't a movie. This man who spent decades performing funerals and discussing his own had moments of confusion and fear in his last days. He wasn't himself—and then he was.

Going home. Letting go. Welcomes. Goodbyes. Experiencing first breaths and last are a part of becoming.

When Sully and I got married, we were broke. My parents' friends swooped in to help by catering the wedding reception. I still regret not having more dancing and wine, but there is a lifetime of dancing and shared dinners with friends to be had. When it was time for Dad to walk me down the aisle, we took a long walk through the church hall before arriving at the back of the sanctuary. He filled me with love, encouragement, and assurance. He reminded me that he was not a great dancer, and begged I take it easy on the father-daughter dance.

We laughed, weaving through the reception area where tables were set and a buffet prepared, and then I spotted a silver cup of beef jerky. The sticks were slender and individually wrapped. A silver cup did not help glamorize the bouquet of meat sticks. I stopped Dad and bemoaned, "I can't do it. I know we are on a budget, but we are *not* serving gas station jerky today."

I am sure I was nervous and flustered about more than jerky.

Dad said, "Okay, what do you want to do?"

He didn't solve it. He asked what I wanted. Such a simple powerful question before escorting me down the aisle.

I smiled, hid the silver cup under a skirted table holding family photos and we continued our walk to meet Sully.

At our annual Christmas party, I often put out sticks of jerky in a silver cup.

No one ever asks why or complains.

Boundless becoming.

Bar-tailed godwits are shorebirds, waders, and wanderers. Several years ago, scientists implanted tracking devices to follow the birds' migratory patterns. They discovered bar-tailed godwits travel over seven thousand miles for more than a week without stopping. No breaks for rest, eating or recovery. This species flew a distance twice as far as scientists previously perceived migratory birds could fly.

These birds travel from Alaska to New Zealand in March and make the return trek in September. The birds sleep in flight by shutting down one part of their brain at a time. They learn the rotation of the sky. Their migration is a nonstop distance many did not think was possible for any animal or fowl. We limited their capacity by our assessments of size and strength, but we never altered their ability. We did not understand what these birds could endure and become until we studied their patterns and travelled their journeys. Scientists are still trying to understand how these creatures complete their quest. Our discovering begins with acknowledging they can do it.

We limit life.

We limit ourselves. We limit others.

Why?

Insecurity. A lack of understanding. An unwillingness to grow. Exhaustion. Fear. Maybe we find comfort in where we are, regardless of whether or not it is a healthy state to be.

Social envy persisted long before the digital age. We may grumble in our hardship and moan of perceived entitlement. Instead, let's stop tying their win to our loss. In fact, remove the term "loss" and change it to "not yet." Your dream is becoming. It is in progress.

Move their good to your grace. Their joy is not your prison. You have the freedom to become. If you are frustrated when others are moving further, fill yourself with whatever is true, noble, reputable, authentic, compelling, and gracious. Seek the best and the beautiful for yourself and others.

Death is not a limit if you lead a life of legacy building.

Don't limit love or kindness.

Don't limit truth, integrity, and laughter.

Spend time connecting instead of correcting.

Eliminate injustice and hate.

We tend to tolerate ugly words and ineptness in elected officials. Why? What is our threshold? What is a reasonable limit? Politicians pass bills they have never read. We accept bare minimums and become like a school teaching to standards instead of excellence. We can change the tone and begin transformation.

We do so when we change limits within ourselves.

What five words best describe you?

The words will change as you grow in grit, grace, hope, and love.

Do not let today's descriptors limit all you can become.

Your fall is not your failure.

Their win is not your wreck.

Keep going. Persist. Be open. Meet with folks to garner creative ideas for fulfilling a dream.

Stop giving truth to the lies in your head.

We limit uses whether we are feeling mighty and unstoppable or meek and unlovable.

A research team led by The Georgia Institute of Technology developed a new treatment to thwart cancer using gold rods. We award Olympians gold medals and exchange golden bands as an outward symbol of love and commitment. According to a dearth of commercials narrated by old, seasoned actors, gold is a solid investment. Gold nanorods, consisting of gold atoms, may stop cancer's progression. Gold is used in coins, medals, electronics, jewelry, and a radioactive isotope of gold is used in treating cancer.

There are more magnificent uses for gold.

There are more magnificent uses for you and me.

You're welcome.

Once in a while when I visit schools it reminds me of entering a prison. Likely inadvertent or inattentive rather than an intentional design, the signage and security can feel familiar. Experience necessitates barriers to entry. In some communities, a walk to a school or the district's headquarters is uninspiring and weakens creativity when the whole purpose is beautifully shaping wondrous becoming.

At a local school, the first sign you see is a warning. Dire. Bold. Cue the music – dunt, dunt, dunnnnnnnnnt. Instead of welcoming everyone to a place of higher learning and discovery in the arts, science, math, and technology, it reads:

NO

DROPOFFS

PARKING

STOPPING

SERIOUSLY, NO

This means YOU!

Emergency vehicles may need access before, during or after school.

Set a good example for students.

NO STOPPING

You've arrived - excited, scared, timid, hopeful, curious.

Here's your welcome – **NO, NO, NO!**

It is a good school with good people. "No" is not who they are or what they offer. The sign for all who enter is a bold, capitalized, "NO" with an exclamation point emphasizing the severity and potential yelling of this command. Parking for emergency vehicles is important. We want to honor safety. Let's do so while sharing our brand, ideals, and goals. Let families, students, and educators know they are welcome, valued, and needed.

This "SERIOUSLY, NO" signage is in the center of the parking lot entrance.

An important adage is omitted, "We're glad you're here."

Imagine if they offered words declaring, "YES, you are walking into something wonderful."

Leaders and teachers care deeply about the whole child, but somebody got fired up about improper parking issues and now the first impression is punishment, emergency vehicles, and strict security. No one is there to greet you. This is how a day begins for families, students, and teachers. Imagine what could happen if we changed the signs.

What if carpool drop-off had inspirational messages and teachers who high-fived and cheered for students as they headed in? What if messages of hope, love, and expectation continued throughout the school on placards and in voices? Instead of "No parking" or "No cell phones," a day could begin with "Yes."

WELCOME!
COME ON IN. WE NEED YOU.
TOGETHER WE WILL WONDERFULLY CHANGE THE WORLD.
(Yes, we shouted that!)

They may still include instructions for parking and protection. But, instead of greeting people with what they *can't* do, begin with all they *can* do.

Another nearby school has similar concerns posted in parking lots and carpools. Years ago, a child was killed getting hit by carpool driver, heightening safety alarms. A new sign provides instruction:

PLEASE SQUEEZE VERY CLOSE TOGETHER.

Below the text is an image of two cartoon cars - different colors, nestled close to each other. In this message of safety, the school is conveying who we ought to be as people - in parking lots and in our daily togetherness.

Homes, corporations, stadiums, schools, houses of worship, apps, and sites are places we gather. They offer billowing hope, refuge, escape, possibility, and beginnings, and yet it is often difficult to find a sign of welcome, and in some cases, even a bathroom.

Who is to blame? Me. We.

All of us are accountable for how we receive, embrace, and usher in.

What is the first thing people see when they enter your office, home or heart?

Does it convey the message you want delivered?

Hospitals have soothing music, cool air, and compelling art, but what offers the most impact are the people who greet and the ease of finding where you need to go.

Our friend Joe used to welcome neighbors with a flag. If the Irish flag was flying, his pool was open. No need to ask, just come on back. You'd find him reading a paper, ready to talk about world events while offering an icy gin and tonic or a creamy scoop of ice cream.

The initial walking in is hard. We don't know if we'll be welcomed. Do you ever do a little dance with a friend or spouse jostling for position? "No, you go ahead. Go first." It might be somewhere familiar, like a pediatrician's office, and if you are heading in with concern and worry, the welcome you receive can change your perspective and parenting. Imagine if doctors' offices had messages of comfort on the wall. Not hundreds of guideposts creating sensory overload which might be a tad chaotic like an enthusiastic kindergarten classroom experience – but just a few assurances. Technology enables messages to update and evolve. Consistency could soothe anxious patients and families. Healing might begin before the doctor arrives. It is a welcome change to a cold room, long wait, and stale images.

As we grow, if we learn well, we become comfortable in the uncomfortable. We courageously go in.

Be thoughtful as you tread in someone else's pain.

Movies and reality shows at times depict visiting jail or prison as a bit sexy or exciting. It is not. Being a prosecutor requires interviewing witnesses and sometimes they are incarcerated. It is a peculiar experience to take a case to trial where the victim and defendant are both repeat offenders. Juries, judges, and attorneys can view them as a lost lot. All of us - you, me, experts, and our elected officials - have too few conversations about bail, repeat offenders, mandatory sentencing, poverty, and ways to morph incarceration to reformation and restoration.

I remember talking to a young man in jail, he was likely ten years younger than I was at the time. He had a gruff edge and snarly attitude. He didn't want to reveal anything. I understood. The other prisoners knew why we were meeting. Getting vulnerable and honest with me meant a torturous existence for him. It was an armed robbery, aggravated assault case. He was there when it happened, arrested on other charges.

I had picked the wrong location and strategy for us to connect. He let me know this the moment I entered the room. Cold, a single table, three metal chairs. I said a quick hello and launched into the facts, offering leniency on his charges in return for doing the right thing. I was focused on my case, the victim, and her family, not realizing the potential for helping this prisoner. Still in his teens, statistics would argue his locale meant his lot was cast. I had an opportunity to do more than bring justice in a courtroom. At one point, he jumped up and started yelling, threatening me, and refusing to say another word. I was startled but didn't let my fear show. A wonderful, muscled detective with me stood up too. He stayed calm, unrattled by the unraveling. I didn't know other prisoners were walking by. I missed the signs. I would have to talk with him again in a safer setting, not for me, but for him. I needed to think more about the ramifications for testifying long after he was released.

I officially became an Assistant District Attorney when a letter arrived in my hospital room. A consummate late bloomer, I had complications and a cracked jaw from wisdom teeth extractions. I had a good interview but could not follow-up as my fever spiked. On the third day of my hospital stay, a hand-written letter arrived from the District Attorney. It said, "Get well. Your job and team await. Congratulations on becoming an Assistant District Attorney." A welcome and an affirmation.

As prosecutors, I don't think we spoke often enough about the sacredness in holding such power. Criminal charges, sentencing recommendations, witness interviews, speaking to victims who are handcuffed to a hospital bed because they are charged with a crime, attending an autopsy and later watching the coroner testify using the same pen he used to point out stab wounds and defensive cuts, these were experiences I had to choose how to handle. What would I become? How would they shape me?

People give us signs and we ignore them to our peril. A friend makes us feel good, we connect and our longing for more makes us overshare. Alcohol and long days of work can also prompt oversharing. We give a piece of ourselves and they devour it. You tell a boss about a diagnosis or medical scare. You call a friend and share your worry about paying for college and the mortgage. Everybody else sees your shiny self and stately manor. We want to let people in. We need to share our hurts to become whole. In a moment, we are authentic, raw, and wide-open. Listeners can hurt or heal.

Look for the signs. Run to people you can trust. Stop seeking validation from those who wound. It only takes one person to fully love and empower us to become. If you can count a few more, it is far beyond most. With their abiding presence, we break free from the lie of believing we are not enough when we are fully ourselves.

Everyone one of us knows the fear of belonging:

If they fully know me, will they love me?

You will know you are home when the answer is a resounding, "Yes."

Awaken to hurt. Don't deny yourself grace. We let our guard down, share a burden, and friends start loving on us. Bringing meals, running errands, calling and texting, they cover us with love but suddenly we feel worse because of guilt. Let people love on you. Let them serve. Let them welcome your pain with arms of empathy and hearts of humility. It's okay to gently say when it is enough but stop feeling bad when warrior women and mighty men rally an army to attend. There is no competition for sufficient levels of pain, grief, and hardship. Weariness is when love brings rest, if you let it in.

My beautiful friend Holly taught me this as she battled breast cancer. Through chemo, baldness, and bad days, she would ask about my pain. I wouldn't give in. I'd insist, "Let's focus on you." She'd lovingly advise, "Let's focus on us."

She extravagantly loves. She heals while healing.

There are irritants. There are people who pray to announce gossip instead of calling on grace. They bring dishes and espouse reasons for why bad things happen. An initial text mentions your pain and twists into a lengthy look into their own aching past. Keep them away. They are not worthy of your precious pain.

Because my dad was a beloved minister who frequently visited in homes and hospitals, people wanted to come see him when he got sick. If anyone stayed too long and tried to turn the visit into a counseling session, we told Dad to pretend he was asleep. We would give him exaggerated signs behind the visitor so we could gently announce,

"Thank you so much for coming. It looks like Dad needs rest."

He did.

We all do.

Go ahead and pretend you're asleep, unless there are no other adults around and three-year-olds have access to scissors and lipstick.

Final Thoughts on Becoming

One evening I was leaving basketball practice with our daughters. The league convenes on courts in a local large church. As we headed out, we noticed several food trucks, and I thought, "What a great idea to welcome people by offering dinner to go."

Families were coming out of choir programs, meetings, and basketball practices to converge on the blessing of not cooking. As my girls begged and tugged to see the offerings, I started giggling. The girls wanted to know why. I wouldn't say. I snapped a picture to send to a few friends. It was a sign painted on the side of the meatball truck. There it sat in a church parking lot with a proud, misplaced message,

"You won't regret putting our ballz in your mouth."

And the people said, "Amen?"

Does a "z" make an "s" look wimpy?

Should I change my name to Zarah?

We headed to the car as I pondered this and wondered what would become of dinner.

Your unshakable, paramount identity is accepting you are beautiful, loved, and blessed. This is who we are; what we become depends on if we plant this truth in someone else. This is a light of life.

CHAPTER TWELVE

HOPE

Hope is the sight of a star.
Hope is sure-footing on an uncertain path.
Hope is our survival.

We have this hope.

We have this hope that says, "Yes, it will be" to those who doubt.

It defies the obvious and understood.

It is unyielding, unbound, and assuring.

It is a mother facing unbearable pain who sews memories believing they will carry on.

It is a family moving from preventative to palliative care who somehow finds a path to sing, laugh, and love.

It is a living hope in a valley of desolation and danger. It is gives rise to endurance, empowering progress when there is little sign of improvement. Through hope - with hope - we know good takes time. With hope, we thrive.

Hope is what we cling to in abuse, unrest, and outbreaks. It is not a childish whim or wish. It is a belief that suffering will cease and joy will come. Hope is alive in barren lands. We are breathless witnessing hope in desolation.

Hope surrounds us. Joined with grit, grace, and love, it is infinite in influence. Scientists acknowledge its power in the process of healing. Its absence is a poverty of mind and spirit. Hope is more than an optimistic outlook. It is not sunshine, rainbows, daydreams, or delusions. It is a positive view of the future captivating our present state. Hopeful people believe things will get better, although outcomes may not occur as expected. Hope brings assurances of something greater than what we planned. Disappointments come but with hope we are not weighed down in a tumble of despair. With hope, we keep our eyes on the prize. We mourn losses, suffer, yet persist in positive paths. Giving up hope for one goal does not mean we lose hope for life. A situation can seem hopeless when death is near, a friendship breaks or a house burns down. We can hope to win the lottery and contend everything will be better with that win, but this is false hope. Authentic hope fills you with joy and peace. It is a confident knowing, assurance, and expectation. It is the reason Anne Frank believed people are still good, while she remained in hiding. It is why Nelson Mandela could foster reconciliation after twenty-seven years in prison. It is a reason why, regardless of position, power or pain, one can live a whole, abundant, robust, rewarding life.

What if we get what we hoped for and find it is nothing like we thought it would be?

Letting go of a dream means releasing the hope *for something*. This is different than putting your hope *in something*. I may hope for the growth of a start-up company and it never actualizes. Moving on to another opportunity is letting go of a goal. My faithful, true hope is more than focusing on isolated outcomes. Authentic hope is far greater than these.

A cry in the dark. A search for the plunger.

"I clogged the toilet going number three."

Hopeless and helpless can start right here. Sure, these twins of gloom appear with the big letdowns of life - illness, betrayal, loneliness. They also grow from seemingly innocuous ground cover, evolving into suffocating vines that slowly destroy a sturdy tree. A great day can flip upside down, or a tad bit hard day can shift into absolutely awful because of one more mess piling on. This is why when times are good, when life is swimming along in sunny happiness, we need to remember how everything worked out. Eventually all became okay. We need to recall the good feelings and joyful times. When we think something horrendous is going to happen and it doesn't, acknowledge your gratitude and joy in the moment. You have found hope.

Savor hope.

We all have expectations, some grand, some just getting through. A magnificent whole life is one where we embrace the hope of *"even if."* We believe something better will happen. We have hope things will improve, but even if things do not go as planned, we will still proceed in grit, grace, hope, and love.

An *"even if"* mindset takes practice and support. Mourn losses, cry out, ask for help. Serve others and know you are not alone in a hurtful place. When hopeful veers to hopeless, get away from those who thrive in negativity and theatrics. Focus on the good in yourself, in others, and in the moment. All is not lost in a loss. You can set out alone, but you won't be alone. Hope will come. Love will abide. Sometimes we just need to go to bed. As my warrior friend Holly says, "We all need one pajama day. Two in a crisis means you might not revive or shower for a while, but one pajama day is a good way to re-group and gain perspective."

Get off social media if seeing someone's name or post hurts.

Stop longing to be appreciated by an anonymous mob.

Try doing something unrelated to the loss. Perform small, healthy acts.

Don't seek to destroy others, although perhaps some could use a good finger wag and instructive commentary. Tearing others down is what tears us apart.

You may want to linger in the ache of your loss. That's okay. Stay a while if you need to, but just not so long that you lose yourself in darkness. Hope begins to soothe our sores while we are still grieving. We simply need to let hope in.

I know the heavy anguish of a heart so broken it feels every breath is pushed against the weight of a thousand sumo wrestlers. It hurts. It seems we should be able to move on – we're not necessarily depressed, but are lurching around, crouched over, saddled with sadness. We are grappling with forgiveness and sorrow. We need time to break free. One quote about forgiveness doesn't rouse us. A quip on the mystery of faith doesn't snap us back to reveling in joy. But hope is quietly, steadily pressing us forward with resilience. Hope breaks through our fear. Hope massages a body paralyzed by pain. Hope churns with grit, grace, and love, forming a restorative balm to heal a weary soul.

Hope is awkward and awesome. It prevents second hand stress.

With grit, grace, love, faith, and gratitude, an ardent rationalist can have hope.

A few years ago, our friends had a beautiful wedding in a chapel nestled in the woods. Guests sat on dark, carved pine pews as light from candles and the sun streamed through to soften the late afternoon service. Pictures of the family posing in front of waterfalls and moss-covered rocks captured the idyllic day.

All looked serene and beautifully appointed in the photos, except for the third strap. In every picture with beloved Aunt Bubby, she is garbed in a light blue gown, turned to the side with three white straps hanging on her arm. Looking at each image, my friend's gaze zoomed on the wide bands of white. One for a bra, one for a slip or Spanx®. But what was the third strap for?

Maybe it was a harness of hope.

Hope encircles us with support. It is a unique cornerstone for every individual. Some may argue hope is an ethereal aspect of life, not a sturdy main or major idea. However, this perspective fails to fully see the work of hope and the health of hope flourishing in a bountiful, whole life.

I think of moments when a father or mother holds a stethoscope and hears the heartbeat of their deceased daughter in a thriving young man. With a transplant, we revive hope. To hear a heartbeat again is to feel the rhythm of hope.

On August 28, 1963, Martin Luther King, Jr. spoke at a hallowed spot to kindle a dream and the fierce urgency of now. He showed us how to carve stones of hope out of mountains of anguish, impediments, and despair.

We must put these stones of hope in our hands to keep hope alive.

What do you hold in your hand today?

We Sullivans keep a bowl filled with things to hold on our kitchen counter. In the bowl are small symbols of grit, grace, hope, and love. Everything in the bowl is meant for your palm and is intended for sharing. Hold it for as long as you might need it. Listen for the time you should give it away. We strengthen our grit, grace, hope, and love when we share them.

A few of the items in the bowl are stones given to me by my friend, Jada. They are beautiful, smooth, and carry the word "Hope" etched on one side. I keep a stone of hope in my car so I can grab it and share it with the kids. I promise not to hurl it on any rough rides.

What do you hold to keep hope alive?

Hope is larger than our lot. It is the indomitable, venturesome wings of love pushing us to do what seems so little and redeems so much. It is choosing to feed people today, even though more will come hungry tomorrow. It is deciding to light a heart or home nearby, even if you are tired, thirsty, and heartbroken. Hope is unfailing love holding us tight as life pummels us with pain. Hope brings us through hardships to hallelujahs. Hope is radical, radiant light in darkness. Hope stands in between, letting us hold the truth while hearing the lie saying we are nothing special. Hope sees truth and stirs us to share uncompromising kindness. Hope says "yes" when the tired and insecure contend it cannot be. Hope braids into a cord with strands of faith and love and is not easily broken. People of hope care for others – the loveable and unlikeable, the captivating and irritating. You and me. They sit with the lonely. They continuously care for the poor - those impoverished financially and spiritually. They offer grit, grace, hope, and love in seemingly hopeless spaces.

A whole life cradles the isolated, least, and lost with hope.

Hope is here for us because despite social media evidence to the contrary, *we are isolated, least, and lost.*

You will find hope on a highway outside of Winston Salem, North Carolina when on a late July afternoon thousands of sunflowers are blooming. Hope plants seeds by the roadside without ever knowing what will bloom or who will be blessed by the view. Hope tills a perilous, rocky soil and scatters seeds, believing beauty will grow. Hope nurtures and nourishes.

Hope is why Johnny Cash cut a live album in a prison.

With worldly turmoil and global threats, we may feel powerless and hopeless. We are not. We are never without hope.

Hope springs when we tend to one another.

When my husband was a little boy, he'd race home from school to his grandparents' house. There he'd find a snack, warmth, and people who loved him.

His grandfather, an old solider and cook, offered quiet presence and assurance. His grandmother first doted as her grandson rushed through the door, and then set him free to swim and play. They parented differently than we do and followed a different journey than our own, but they surely loved this little boy. A small window of time in the course of a life, it provided an expectation of hope and comfort. As a teenager or when home from college and feeling misunderstood, my husband could go to his grandparents' home. He didn't need a key. The carport screen door was open. He could come, stay or go whenever he chose. He was always welcome. Always loved.

Our restless souls cause us to wander. We seek nurture from places of discouragement. We fill holes with temporal comforts. We are unwilling to be still and let things be.

We are called to build communities of hope. Homes of hope.

Grandma and grandpa offered their grandson jelly and butter sandwiches after a long swim.

We can offer hope with a smile.

We will not always have answers to a crisis at hand.

We can bring hope with five phrases:

Are you okay?

I'm so sorry.

Count on me, call on me.

I'm here.

How can I help?

Hope is the willingness to wait for answers. Hope is the power of presence.

Hope lives next door.

She is a friend and wise mother of three who embodies Hope, for it is her name. In an age of vast and fast technology, we bring each other flowers from the yard, soup and bread for a weary soul, and share advice on caring for kids and parents. She is a renowned artist who takes time to stoop low at eye level to talk with our youngest about her crayon renderings. She comforts me when obstacles crop up. "Sarah, it is your first time, and it is your child's first time. Find a way to laugh as you guide each other." Her wisdom nurtures me.

Good neighbors see you braless and shoeless as you usher kids out the door and understand why you smile and cross your arms over your chest in lieu of a welcoming wave. They come in when laundry is piled high on the table and a random dog or covey of children, not belonging to your abode, are racing through the house. They bring hope, knowing when to sit, when to go, and when to roll up their sleeves and tackle a pile or a streaming tear.

Hope prevails in the darkest hours and scariest times.

Hope is an essential part of our reply when people wonder why and how we are able to carry on with joy. Hope and joy integrally entwine, laced with the silk of gratitude and remembrance.

Hope empowers us to find joy as we guide each other through the unexpected and arduous.

Hope is a choice. We can find hope every day. It is easily missed and unacknowledged. Recognizing hope, holding it with gratitude, transforms impossible and improbable to *imagine me.*

People and motion activate hope. Color comes in. Light is welcomed home. We view grays and glooms of life as spaces where hope is lost. But they are where hope begins. Just as a hue of gray in a room makes other colors come vibrantly alive, hope brings us to life when shadows form in the absence of light.

Where do you find hope?

Can you name it?

Do you find hope in actions, presence, or prayer?

In a vexing week with various stressors and concerns I found these hopes:

"I love you."
"Come join my tribe."
"The bosom is here if you need it."
"Call me."
"Unpack your bag of rocks, friend,
and feel good about doing it."

"You are not alone."
"I'm praying for you."
"Let us carry you, lift you up, massage your aches,
wipe your tears, encourage, and love you."

Oh, how easy it is to miss hope and holy ground.

In communities, we have the opportunity every day to give and receive hope. Like grace and love, we often miss it. When my friend Joe died, his family found his writings scattered throughout the house. Whether scribbled on scraps or listed on a legal pad, Joe's words offered comfort for those who remained. He had an art for taking turgid styles and bringing them into picturesque, powerful headlines. One piece looked like he periodically returned for additions. The title read, "My Places in the Sun." I leave his places with his family, but wonder what you would inscribe?

Your places in the sun are places of hope. They are people of hope. Your place could be a lap or lawn. Maybe it's a meal and those seated around the table.

It is there that you feel the presence of love.

My friend Celeste puts it this way,

"Hope is having you for a friend."

There is the hope in a meaningful conversation. There is hope when we can talk about our differences and common ground. There is hope in a warm bath.

My mom recently told me a story about a little girl who accidentally locked herself in a bathroom at a birthday party. Did she cry? Jiggle the door furiously? Maybe. Will Rogers said, "When you find yourself in a hole, quit digging." For this little girl, hope took hold. Her parents found her safe and sound - taking a bath.

When we face fear, we need authentic hope. Our daughter Gabrielle hopped out of the car to head into school one morning and called, "Bye, I love you. I can't wait to get home and tell you about the great day I'm going to have." She began her day with hope. Confident in joyful expectation. Her view gives her strength when trouble comes. Why do we let go of this childlike faith? As adults, we see the hope of a great day on the horizon as a Pollyanna perspective instead of a whole life directive. We fall into the "too trap" –

I'm too old.

I'm too young.

It's too late.

I'm too tired.

I'm too busy.

I'm too stressed, worried, and overwhelmed.

One of the saddest things we do to each other is exacerbate false limitations. When our son, Jack, was in eighth grade he thought about playing baseball. He had not played since he was five, having switched to lacrosse, football, and track. He came home from school and said, "I wish I could play baseball this spring, but I'm too old to start now. It's too late."

A nourishing, vibrant local baseball league agreed, or at least that was the message conveyed. The rebuff was offered with an affirming nod, agreeing in the sigh for this is seemingly how it is, but it does not have to be so. I've seen this pattern repeated with other children who want to try a new sport. They train all summer and then do not make the team. We offer no alternatives. We echo there are not enough positions and far too many players who picked the sport at age seven. They play in school and travel leagues.

Think of what our world would miss if every ground-breaking scientist, generation changing writer, mischievous and magical chef, or freed prisoner poet who advocates for the voiceless thought it was too late.

Deny the *tyranny of too*.

It is not too late to pick up a ball and glove and play.

It is not too late for you to be beautifully become.

There is nothing you are too late to do at fourteen. Go. Grab hold. Begin. Listen to the learned and loving. Ignore cynics who lack light and don't carry your best interests at heart. What if you wake up as fourteen becomes thirty in the blink of an eye, realizing you had not begun what you were called to commence?

Everything can begin at age fourteen.

Everything can begin at fourteen, forty or eighty. Maybe your triathlon times are slower. Maybe your dunks land without a rousing alley-oop, but there is no stopping all you are called to be if you would only quit limiting yourself. Let hope begin the wondrous you within. Who cares if your brush strokes are shaky? Those trembling hands may spark breath into lost lives because of what people see in your art.

You breathe in and out, therefore you are called to do and be. Wonderful works await. It is what you want and what the world needs. Do it and bring light to just one person who may in turn light a home, a village, a nation. Hope dawns with you. You are the one.

Arm your aim with hope and mercy, not pessimism and hate. Mercy is offering compassion when you could choose to punish. Give yourself mercy and hope. Offer it to others and inspire dreams. Choose to live a whole life. Do not wait on wonder because you need to lose twenty pounds or your finances are tight or your body is bent-over.

Resources abound. Work a little bit every day on what you really want. Tune out time wasters. Use apps for accountability and research. Tell a few trusted friends about your goals and listen to their dreams in turn. Carry each other. Check in - "How is the dream coming along?" Send texts of support - "I hope today you got a pocket of time and break-throughs." We lose our way with distractions and darkness but must not lose sight of hope. Age and stage are primary excuses for what never becomes. "Too" qualifiers fuel the lie. Hopeless is a lie. Unfailing love is an exquisite truth.

This creative, radical, beautiful dream of yours can happen. It may morph a bit wonky before you see the wonderful. Let it flourish into something dazzling, delicate, ferocious, and fun.

We carelessly limit children.

We foolishly limit ourselves.

Why? Doubt is an easier default. We discourage the very things that would bring us joy because capturing our bliss may involve some tumbles. Yes, you might fall while everyone is watching. Not everyone will notice. Their eyesight is getting weaker and they have their own dreams and diversions to focus on. We accept false narratives when we are wholly capable of achieving more than we see in ourselves and in others. Hope is exponential potential. We are in this quest for a whole life together. We are called to encourage one another and build each other up. Allow people the freedom to demonstrate they are able before quashing their abilities. Love them through the tries and trials. Love yourself, too.

Astound your insecurities by growing in grit, grace, hope, and love. Face the roars of crowds and monsters – both real and imagined. Whispering hope walks into fear and says, "You can do it. Let's try again."

When our son Henry was little, we would read *Where the Wild Things Are* by Maurice Sendak. When we reached the page where the monsters gnashed their terrible teeth, Henry would plead for us to hurry past *the roars*. The roars – those horned monsters – frightened him, but in my lap, holding my hand, Henry could go on. He had assurance in the face of fear. We tackled those roars together.

An oft repeated African proverb expresses it takes a village to raise a child. I think it takes many tribes. A tribe may grow old along with you, rocking hope on porches through laughter, loneliness, births, babes, teens, aging parents, anxiety, changing jobs, illness, times of less, and times of more. Tribes arm you for life's roars. Sometimes your tribe is temporary. Tribes carry hope.

The hope of Harriet and Edna.

On a recent trip to Washington, D.C., hope arose with a woman named Edna. The kids and I spent the morning walking from our hotel to visit The Mall and monuments, finally reaching the Smithsonian National Museum of African American History and Culture. Heading to the entryway, we learned tickets were required and we had none. In those moments, the person in charge of the retractable queue for crowd control holds inordinate power. She told us we could wait in line on the lawn for the next tour. Two more hours, four kids, a hot, sticky day. Definitely a bad combination. We had walked for miles visiting dinosaurs and the larger than life Lincoln, all while talking about this museum. Our youngest, Gabrielle, loves Harriet Tubman and could not wait to see the silk and white lace shawl Harriet received as a gift from Queen Victoria. She longed to be near a piece of her hero – to come close to a warrior's cloth.

Our first tour of the morning was at the Smithsonian National Museum of Natural History. We had one goal: the dinosaurs. We had visited Washington, D.C., a few years earlier but the dinosaur exhibit was closed for restoration. Gabrielle loves dinosaurs. She studies their origins, sizes, and physiques. She enjoys Jurassic set-ups and moves to non-traditional perspectives when she lovingly places dresses and pearls on her blue, stuffed T-Rex named "Queenie." In one room of the museum people are at work - dusting fossils, looking in microscopes. Gabrielle grabbed paper and pen from my purse and made a sign, "I dream of doing this one day. Girl power." She held it up to the window. The women at work never looked up. I understood, for if they did so for every visitor, work would never get done. They didn't see her. It didn't matter. Gabrielle saw herself.

Gabrielle likes to wear dinosaur shirts with skirts and shorts. We often searched the boys' clothing section for dino attire, which meant our daughter did not want to make the purchase. This year, we found shirts encompassing science, dinosaurs, and outer space in the girls' department. The shirts came in an assortment of colors and styles, including a long-sleeve, light pink button-up shirt flanked with small dinosaurs. The world is wonderfully changing.

On her first day of school, two girls made fun of Gabrielle for wearing a dinosaur shirt. We comforted her with grit, grace, hope, and love. We let her decide what to wear on day two. She headed out clothed in another dinosaur shirt and did so on days three and four.

With grit, grace, hope, and love, we march forward to pursue the marvelous parts of ourselves.

With grit, grace, hope, and love, we put pictures of Harriet Tubman and dinosaurs on bedroom doors. We wear knee-high super hero socks with capes flying, purple shorts, and dinosaur shirts while conquering adverbs and times tables.

Thank you, Gabrielle, for helping me see that Harriet's lace is a hero's cape, not a simple shawl. At the age of nine, you are one of my heroes.

And so is Harriet.

Harriet Tubman suffered from horrible headaches, sleeping spells, and possibly seizures – all resulting from a head injury caused by an overseer chasing after another slave. Yet she persisted in hope. She was a nurse, Union spy, and a suffragette. She was a slave who escaped to freedom yet found there was no one to welcome and guide her.

"I looked at my hands to see if I was the same person.
There was such glory over everything. The sun came up
like gold through the trees and I felt like I was in heaven."

Harriet Tubman had to make her own way, and in doing so, she claimed the hope of freeing others. She willingly returned to the place and people who might beat, imprison, and kill her. On her dangerous treks to bring others to freedom, she allowed the evening stars to guide her way. Her work brought no monetary riches, but garnered international fame and the attention of a queen. She pushed people to liberty by echoing the fortitude to keep going,

"If you hear the dogs, keep going. If you see the torches in
the woods, keep going. If there's shouting after you, keep
going. Don't ever stop. Keep going. If you want a taste of
freedom, keep going."

Hope keeps us going.

Hope brings the taste of freedom.

With hope, we overcome.

There is such glory over everything.

We hear stories of what others have done before us, and we are moved to carry on.

Awesome is an over-used, watered-down term. When you see grit, grace, hope, and love at work, you experience awe and wonder. It is awe-inspiring to feel the peace of a restful heart that was once racing and tense. Grit, grace, hope, and love are formidable and marvelous. We easily forget their awe.

We need recollections of joy and hope, particularly when long lines arise and muck up our perspective.

On that summer day in Washington, D.C., we wanted to see things Harriet Tubman held close to her heart. I wavered about an uncomfortable two-hour wait to see artifacts of unbearable suffering, daring hope, and glorious triumph. Seems ridiculous now, but it is a reality we all understand. Exhaustion, heat, and tired bodies need a whisper of hope.

It came.

As I turned to figure out strategies for which of us could stand in line while others got food, a sweet voice behind me said, "I have tickets."

Surely, perhaps just two or three.

I said, "You are so kind, but we need five."

She said, "I have them. You will love this experience."

I was overwhelmed. My tiredness turned to lightness. Her thoughtfulness changed our outlook.

"You are a beautiful blessing," I told the woman as the barrier moved and we were warmly ushered in. I introduced myself and asked her name. She said, "My name is Edna. Can I give you a hug?"

We embraced. I told her, "When you lay in bed tonight wondering if you did something wonderful today, the answer is 'Yes.'"

We headed inside the crisp, cold museum, ready to learn and explore when I stopped to have Team Sully huddle. Right where we were, I wanted us to acknowledge and give thanks for Edna. I knew some of what we would encounter on our tour would be hard to see. Shackles, an auction stone, beautiful people tortured and treated as commodities. Museum visitors descend underground to walk up through stories of oppression and resilience, of love and faith. We needed to walk beside the artifacts in reverent hope and to do so required beginning with gratitude.

In the middle of the lobby, before the welcome desks and under a Richard Hunt sculpture, we gave thanks for Edna, grateful for the unexpected hope to see a piece of Harriet, harsh truths, and beautiful stories.

With Edna, we walked into hope - with hope.

Hope will establish.

"We, the people,
in order to form a more perfect Union,
establish ...."
-*The Preamble to the United States Constitution*

Nations are founded on hope.

Families are built with hope.

Dreams are propelled by hope.

People are designed to harness hope.

Hope inspires and activates, transforming the life we have into a life we want.

Hope lets us build things upon rock bottom. Hope shapes and binds us. Hope helps us heal.

After someone dies, the *firsts* are tough. Hope may be hard to find in such times.

My dad died when I was in my early thirties. We spent every Christmas Day of my life together, and the first December without him hurt. He loved presents, Christmas, and more presents. Even when he was sick and on dialysis, he kept traditions going, putting a bow from a present on his head before guessing, "What could it be?" Even if he knew, the guess was farfetched and silly.

We need more silly.

Someone you love dies and the world whirls on while you shuffle through grief. Sully wished missing my dad meant ushering out certain Christmas songs. Anything by *The Carpenters* or an oft-played classic about drinking beer with an old girlfriend are his least favorite holiday tunes. No luck. I played them all.

A common fear and pain for those who have lost loved ones is that people will forget. Remembering is a blessing. It brings hope. I came home one evening that first December without Dad and noticed an odd light coming from my bathroom. My friend Elizabeth had snuck into the house to place a piece of hope for this hard holiday. It was a pink Christmas tree, filed with twinkling lights.

I pull out this tree every year. It now sits on a dresser in our daughters' room for all the month of December. It is a reminder of hope and the unexpected possibility it brings.

No matter how dark the night, hope is the promise of joy in the morning. It is the assurance of comfort in mourning.

Hope is deliciously absurd. It is the prospect of a wonderful future.

Hope brings pink into a gray world.

In business, hope is not a singularly successful strategy. We must combine hope with acknowledging reality. Hope is integral to hard work. It allows us to claim goals and outcomes, while solving unexpected problems along the way.

You can teach people to hope. It fosters trust, strengthens accountability, and problem-solving. Hope motivates and inspires. It generates energy and a common movement toward the greater good.

With hope, I am able. With hope, we all are able.

Hope is sacred and must be offered with fidelity and integrity.

Hope is sustaining. So is anger. We have the choice of where and how we want to live. The "Placebo Effect" – getting well while thinking you are on medications, when taking none - is a reliance on hope. Some may argue hope is the crux of fairytales and wistful, wishful thinking. Others advise not to get our hopes up, to hope for the best but prepare for the worst. Hope alone cannot be the strategy for work and life, but it is a vital part of the whole.

In a 2013 interview with *The New York Times*, Coach Bobby Knight said, "When I first started coaching, one of the worst things I think I heard was 'It will be O.K.' I would wonder, 'How the hell is it going to be O.K.?' The worst word in the English language is 'hope.'"

I do not believe it is the worst word. It is, however, easier said than understood.

Coach Knight may view hope as a childish observation, like one of my favorite insights from actor Chris Pratt: "You can pour melted ice cream on regular ice cream. It's like a sauce!" I agree, Chris. This bonus makes me happy.

Hope and ice cream are good things. They are, unfortunately, not synonymous.

A mother dies. A child is sick. A friend loses his job. Life's crises rarely happen in isolation.

If H.O.P.E. is an acronym for "Hold On, Pain Ends," what happens when the pain continues?

How do we maintain hope? What do we do when dreams die and hopes are dashed?

Lately, I've thought of a sack.

On display at the Smithsonian National Museum of African American History and Culture is a cotton sack, delicately patched from years of tender care. It is stitched with three colors conveying a family's pain, unfailing love, and abiding hope. Here are the words, just as they are woven on the sack:

> *"My great grandmother Rose*
> *mother of Ashley gave her this sack when*
> *she was sold at age 9 in South Carolina*
> *it held a tattered dress 3 handfulls of*
> *pecans a braid of Roses hair. Told her*
> *It be filled with my Love always*
> *she never saw her again*
> *Ashley is my grandmother*
> *Ruth Middleton 1921"*

She never saw her again.

They are all gone.

Grit, grace, hope, and love soar on.

A little girl's life, stolen and sold away, because evil said her life was not her own. "Evil" is not a term we take lightly. It is one to use when we think about the atrocities of slavery long ago and today.

What would you gather to give your daughter so she will remember grit, grace, hope, and love?

What will last?

How do you have the presence of mind to hope in a hopeless place?

Known today as "Ashley's Sack," this heirloom is on loan from Middleton Place in South Carolina. Found at a flea market in 2007, experts tried to determine its origin. They long to find the family tree of Ruth, Ashley, and Rose.

I paused by the display of this patched cloth, aching for a mother who wanted to give her child a legacy of love, while her little girl was taken and sold. I do not move. For a moment, I have no words for my own children are with me, protected, loved, and safe.

The pieces of Rose – her hair, a dress, pecans – are given with assurance of love always. No matter who or what tore her child away, they could not rip apart a mother's love. This is hope. This is the hope of a whole life.

We do not know if Rose could read or write. Perhaps Ashley braided her mother's hair in the evenings or Rose cradled Ashley and dried her tears with the tattered dress. I wonder if they gathered pecans together, whether forced or by choice, for something about those armored shells holding nourishment inside prompted Rose to place them in a sacred space. Rose filled the sack with symbols of what would never fail.

Rose was a woman, a slave in a world not recognizing her worth as a beautiful, profound person. Filling the sack was an act of defiance, not only because the sack and items therein may have technically belonged to the slave owners, but to show how nothing could destroy her strong faith, hope, and love. With these things, Rose left a legacy far beyond her expectations. The story may have been handed down through the words of women, until Ruth stitched Rose's hope. Ruth etched the words on the fragile fabric, just as generations have stitched hope on aching hearts.

A daughter's cloth. A mother's hope.

My grandmother, Carmen Strange, wrote poetry and so does her daughter Cecily, my mother. Some of Carmen's poems are written from my mother's memory. Carmen died of tuberculosis when Mom was very young. In the 1940s, tuberculosis was one of the leading causes of death. Patients were sequestered to sanitariums, kept away from family to prevent the disease from spreading. As explained in the PBS feature, *The Forgotten Plague: Tuberculosis in America,*

> *"By the dawn of the 19th century, the deadliest killer in human history, tuberculosis, had killed one in seven of all the people who had ever lived. The disease struck America with a vengeance, ravaging communities and touching the lives of almost every family. The battle against the deadly bacteria had a profound and lasting impact on the country. It shaped medical and scientific pursuits, social habits, economic development, western expansion, and government policy. Yet both the disease and its impact are poorly understood: in the words of one writer, tuberculosis is our* forgotten plague.'"

I have nothing belonging to my grandmother – no silver thimble, lace lovingly held, ring she wore, or dress she sewed, but because of my mother, I have her poetry. Some words are written as she remembers them while visiting her mother in the sanitarium. Despite pains and losses no child should bear, my mom wrote the words, preserving the hope within. The poetry is her sack. It is our symbol of hope.

A poem by Carmen Riley.
Written in the Sunnyside Tuberculosis Sanitarium
in the late 1940s, as remembered by her daughter, Cecily.

What goes into this frock that I'm sewing,
Besides a short skirt that leaves panties showing,
With brick brack, embroidery and buttons and such,
And wee bit of lace, not much.
As I fold it and baste in and turn in a seam,
With each careful stitch, I sew in a dream.

Some may contend Ruth's stiches and Ashley's story are tales of fiction. I come from a family of writers and dreamers. I know a fragment of Ruth, for I know the precious gift of mothers passing words of love to their daughters.

I wish I knew more. I wonder how Carmen endured separation from her children. Did she long to fill a sack with symbols of love?

What dreams did she sew for her little Cecily?

I want more, but I have this hope.

I can sew dreams for my daughters. I can share the poems of their great grandmother, grandmother, and me.

We have this hope.

I have a mother, who never had a mom scoop her up in her arms, but she scooped up me. In hard times of parenting, marriage, little money, and tight quarters, she wrote. She writes still.

We have a few pictures from her childhood and a couple of quilts from her bed. Mom encouraged us to sleep with them, use them, let them be well-worn and well-loved. Whether from thrashing around or bedwetting, I remember Mom patching those old quilts. She did not believe in keeping things boxed up.

"Read books and fill them with notes and dog-eared pages."

"Don't save your toys in the box they came in. Take them out and play with them."

And with this, we had a constant assurance:

"There is nothing you can do to ever make me stop loving you."

"But Mom, what if we…." We tried to find a loophole. With whatever bad choice we could concoct, she would not yield.

"I would be sad, very, very sad, but there is nothing you can do to ever make me stop loving you."

We thought we grew up with little in the way of material things. Mom had far less and far fewer to cheer her on.

She had this hope. She has it still.

For hope today, I return to the words of her mother, Carmen:

Work in the Spring

The summer sun was in the sky,
The birds were in the trees,
The woodland was a-quiver
With the busy honey-bees.
The smallest and the largest
Were busy with their work,
The grape-vine swings were calling,
But their duty they couldn't shirk.
First comes work and then comes play,
In summer, fall or spring,
When your work is nicely finished,
Then it's time to swing.

For all my life, I've loved swings. Sully and I went to Napa years ago. At one of the wineries we found a flat, wooden-seat swing, held by long ropes on a grand, old tree. One afternoon, we bought a bottle of wine and sat on a blanket to read and relax. Sully picked a spot near the swing. We had the area all to ourselves. Little did I know he picked the spot so I could swing for as long as I wanted. And so, I did.

Together, we have this hope.

There is a dream to stitch, grace to grow, and love to share.

When the work is finished, it's time to swing.

CHAPTER THIRTEEN

LIGHT AND DARKNESS

In 2002, the *Man in Black* filmed his final music video. Johnny Cash covered the Nine Inch Nails song, *Hurt*. The video begins with Johnny dressed in his legendary black, alone, strumming a guitar with gnarled, old hands. Full of broken thoughts, stains of time, and questions for all we become, Johnny turns a young man's song of drug abuse into a glorious reflection of a whole life.

Trent Reznor's lyrics became Johnny Cash's anthem.

The guitar's soft melody guides us to deeper introspection. A piano strikes the pain of the refrain. Johnny opens the lid of an upright piano and plays a beating question with his index finger.

"What have I become?" He asks his sweetest friend.

When Nine Inch Nails recorded *Hurt*, the sweetest friend was a drug. Here, it is June Carter Cash. Her silent, warm presence affirms her husband's query as a rhetorical question.

It is one worth repeating throughout our whole life.

What have I become?

- Am I where I want to be?
- What will I do with the answers?
- How does darkness and light shape me?
- How do I shed darkness and light?
- What *will I* become?

Rays and shadows ebb us back and forth with images of past and present. There is healing sunlight capturing Johnny's smile as he peers into his abandoned childhood home. There is artificial light filling a stage, illuminating his gifts before thousands of roaring and adoring fans. We can't hear the crowd, but we feel them and the energy of both. In the old reels, Johnny sweats, stands, and rocks through the lyrics of long ago. Now he is seated - older, wiser, tired and grateful, hurting, and healed. He is aware of his mortality. He recognizes the difference between being driven and being called. He sees the hope brought by running to, instead of running from. Fame brings everything and nothing.

Johnny's once nimble fingers are crooked yet pulsating the piano and keeping the rhythm of life's beauty, mess, and excess. The desire for more, his accomplishments, and millions of albums sold, are not bad. His work influenced other legends and inspires still. The contrasting views of old and young, of light and dark, show how surplus will eventually sour and wither. We crave and store a mountain of things. Johnny understands life's bounties are meaningless without love. Despite number one hits, by his mid-thirties, Johnny Cash was a hardcore drug user, divorced, and out of control. The empire of dirt could not save him.

Love did.

Light filled his life.

The video rolls on. Unopened champagne chills. Lobster, caviar, and whole fish fill an empty table. A banquet is readied, but no one is there to partake in the feast. Johnny is seated at one end. His wife June stands above him on a stairway, looking down at him with the love of soul mate who wants to take on and take away all the pain. She cannot. She is alongside him; with her, he continues to create music. He continues to be and become. Instead of sipping wine from a golden chalice, he pours it over the feast. The meal is grand, delicious, and over-the-top. It is a far greater spread than one man can eat, and much will go to waste. His haunting voice, aging eyes, and shaking hands illuminate what is important and what is illusory.

Flood waters rage, symbolizing an actual flood of his childhood and the flood of fame washing, rushing over everything that is real. Babies are cuddled. The House of Cash, now a closed museum, is opened once more revealing broken frames and former treasures lying on the floor. June, his family, faith, and music - these are his loves and joys. They are the light. All the rest is an empire of dirt.

The empire is not inherently corrupt or without reward. It is a mixture of light and dark. Living happens in the hues. Johnny sings, examines his life, and concludes if he could start all over again, he would still choose to be himself.

He sees what is temporal and what endures.

The song ends.

Without a sound, he closes the upright piano, caressing his hands over the lid. Director Mark Romanek keeps the camera on those magnificent hands. Content, comforted, and assured. The black and white keys are covered. He can no longer play. In the stillness, the imagery and music linger in us. Johnny shuts the lid and gently wipes his worn fingers over the smooth polished wood, as if closing a coffin and saying farewell. Then they rest. All is still, calm, and sure. It is finished.

A piano and a guitar underscore the story. These two instruments in the video shine, not showing a single nick of age and wear. They are simple, not evoking opulence or waste for they are played in a song bringing resplendence, reflection, and mercy. They do not sit idle, like the food. Their light is shared by one who knows overwhelming loneliness and unfailing love.

June Carter Cash died May 15, 2003. Johnny died on September 12, 2003.

Naked. Honest. Hurt. Healed. We live in light and dark - the choices made in a beautiful, fractured, authentic whole life. Johnny's interpretation of *Hurt* is an end, offering a beginning.

Breath ceases and what lasts is the light of love.

Music plays on, carried through other artisans.

The Man in Black brings light.

There are simple, great things that are hard to hold and say. Light is simple and complex. We wield swift swords of guilt and shame and offer light with arms of love. In law school, we were taught to begin legal answers with two words: It depends. Here, too, what we bring depends on who we are, whom we serve, and what we wield.

Our lives defy and define darkness. We begin to breathe with light. Leaving our mother's womb, we enter the world helpless, crying to thrive. We grow and worries wind up in the dark. The familiar morphs into an ominous shadow. Light is where we learn to swim, ride a bike, and start school. Dark is where we seek rest, find worry, heighten danger, and become brave. We realize darkness is easier to overcome if we are not alone.

"Come with me," our kids will say to each other as they head to the basement or look for something in the car after darkness falls. Two or more bring light to defeat the darkness.

How often do we lay awake at night fidgeting and anxious, longing to defeat the darkness? Sleep finally comes bringing nightmares, stealing our safety and self-assuredness. Through the restless wrangling, we look for words of comfort. *"It's not real. It was probably something you ate. Next time talk to the nightmare. Change the ending while you are in the story. You have the homework. You can yell for help. You are clothed in the crowd."* Healthy community and trusted connections bring warmth.

With light, we are born anew, shedding prior perceptions, objections, and addictions. We tend to think we are all born just once via our mothers' wombs, when life's richness is our repeating rebirth. We are uprooted from colorless seasons of isolation and gloom and replanted in fresh, vibrant soil. We cast off decay, giving birth to new hues of ourselves. Wholeness rouses with light.

You do not have to be who you used to be. It is okay to be afraid as you burst forth and become. Light sparks in deep fear. Light says, *"Oh, there you are. Let's do this dream. Let's begin this passion's quest. As you are – timid and terrified, you are worthy and able. Let's go!*

Light shifts us into a world of imagination and creativity. Its brilliance distorted in the despair of loneliness, starvation, and the pull of wants and needs. In distinguishing evil from all that is true, noble, just, lovely, and good, we call it darkness. Light originates in darkness. Daybreak rises from night. We cherish light when we stand in darkness. Take a tour of Alcatraz and you'll hear a tale of solitary confinement. Biding time and abating fear in the hole, an inmate would tear a button off his shirt, throw it into the darkness and search. Hands become our eyes when we cannot see. We seek restoration in finding what is lost.

We live, move, exist, persist. Darkness and light drive our view. They are internal forces with external influences. As we read more, question authority, and move through life, discovering, discerning, and questioning, darkness and light alter character, aims, and actions.

Darkness manipulates and covers. Light invigorates, sculpts, and mends.

Light leads us home. Darkness pulls us away from all we are called to be.

Light puts your hand in mine and mine in yours. Together, we try. We launch. We become in the middle of all the unknown.

We carry each other.

We do this when I dust off the soot of self-doubt and you do the same.

We are strangers who form a human chain to save treasures in a fire or a family caught in a riptide. We build gardens to feed senior citizens. We serve the homeless for a reception when a wedding is abruptly cancelled. We run races, coordinate parades, and raise funds to finance dreams and find cures. We use social media to answer needs - calls for diapers, food, legal help, water purifiers, or foster families. We lead people to safety as bullets fly and fires rage. "We" means you and me. Your light is unique and exquisite offering more good than you can imagine and more positive outcomes than you can possibly see.

Light is coffee bought for a stranger. Light is showing up and saying, "You don't have to worry about this, we've got it." Light is the illumination of love.

With light, we leap. Your jump may start on a high perch in a canyon and mine might cross a threshold, but they are both powerful and do not need comparison or delineation. Light is the joy of the leap and companionship in the landing.

We jump into the hard work of love. Through light, I love you as I love myself. What does that mean? I love myself by knowing I am imperfect and enough, right now, in this place, time, and condition. I may want more, but I recognize my meaning is not tied to a goal or a "do better." I honor space, yours and mine. I see you are wounded and worthy too. With self-love and care, I dump comparison, envy, and fear. I claim and exclaim, "This has to stop." I get help. I start over. I believe you can also begin again. I recognize choices and consequences. In seeking vibrant, whole lives, you and I don't have to plead for respect or explain ourselves. We lead and live in grit, grace, hope, and love. We do it in a messy, imperfect, fabulous, and frustrating fashion. Light listens. Light asks, "What can I do?" Light shows up at door steps, jail cells, hospice care, and holidays. Light forgives, serves aching people, feeds hungry souls, and welcomes interruptions. Light calls for the courage to reach out with a text to share - "Thank you," "I'm thinking of you," or "Shall we discuss how my boobs are enveloping into my lap?"

Light laughs.

It dances.

There is fundamental light and darkness - delineated lines of good and evil. We want to live in light, but darkness is captivating and confusing. Bias, childhood, community, racism, finances, and uneasiness alter our lenses of love or hate. We are good people, but bad things happen. We make poor choices to get immediate gratification. We lie by omission without contrition. Danger lurks in dark alleys and in the of light day. Darkness is not instantaneous misery. Sun drenched deserts and desolate dry lands long for dark clouds and rain. There is dreaded darkness in the light of the sun. With all this confusion of darkness and light, we justify wrong and claim it is right.

The light we seek is an inside job. With light, we do not hurt people. We heal.

Before the invention of electricity, people worked until darkness and only then rested. There were set times to shut down, sleep, and awaken, all fueled by the rising and setting of the sun. Technology extends life, health, and the work day. Light from our devices improves our lives but interrupts sleep, intimacy, and conversations. In our hand, we hold life-giving light and shift it into an anchor of darkness with just a few swipes.

Nightfall is not our downfall. Delicious dinners, dancing, tender exchanges, and lying on a blanket looking at the stars are splendid joys night brings. Nights are not always scary. There are evenings filled with wide-eyed anticipation - the excitement of the "before." Aviator and inventor Orville Wright once shared, "I got more thrill out of flying before I had ever been in the air at all - while lying in bed thinking about how exciting it would be to fly."

Light is realizing how exciting it would be.

The contrasting darkness is not the loss of sunshine, but the absence of hope. It is the dearth of despair. It is vast, malignant, and strangling. It is small and cunning. It is quick, passive aggressive quips. It is us at our worst. It is our self-entitlement, indulgence, and aggrandizing

We are drawn to light. We are pursued by darkness.

How we respond to failures and not getting what we want exhibits our acceptance of light or darkness.

We espouse there is clarity between good and evil, and yet as prosecutors, my old boss District Attorney J. Tom Morgan taught us, "If you want to see an image of the boogie man, look in the mirror." He was right. We are all capable of good and evil. Who and what will you be? Whom and what will you serve?

All of us, regardless of political party and position, must quash hate. We do so with light and love. Spewing taunts and ridicule in reply only furthers anger. We must have the courage to speak love, with love. We must listen to pain. We need to understand the voids in darkness leading to hate-filled torches in the night.

Darkness is ignorance. Darkness is awareness and failing to act. It is where we crush folks with punitive posts and expect positive outcomes.

In silence, we hear darkness and look for light.

Light is present, even when we cannot see. Light ignites when love holds on in dark spaces. People get progressively better with light. Light shows us what is ahead and assures what we can leave behind. Darkness and light are relatives. Both sit at your table, changing moods in an instant or by inches.

For our whole lives, we must see people with a wider lens on their pain and suffering instead of myopically focusing only on what they say, overlook or neglect.

Backspace, backspace, backspace, backspace.

These are strokes of light.

You are a needed, beautiful light.

To someone today, you are light if you choose to elucidate grit, grace, hope, and love. Empathy, compassion, kindness, patience, and self-control are conduits of light.

Our oldest Jack is tall, broad, and strong. He is a warrior because he wields empathy and wisdom to stand in between. If he sees an older kid picking on a younger one, he stands in between. If he sees a guy who disrespects women lurching over a friend, he stands in between. He doesn't do so with clenched fists. Sometimes folks do not see it happening. We do. He uses his gifts and strengths for good. He is light.

So are you.

Light empowers us to stand in between. Light replaces hate with love. It removes the veil, conquers the terrifying. With light, love is visible, energetic, held, and shared.

With light, I show who I am. I see who you are. In pursuing a whole life, I do not run from light's truth. I am thankful for the illumination. Light allows us to address hate in our hearts, including self-hatred, so we can fully, powerfully, and restoratively love others.

Bringing light, holding a candle, is not a small matter. Life is trying and tiring. It is comprised of joys, pains, laughter, and weird in between time. We hold a candle so others may safely lie down and rest. We raise it so they can soar and run. A tiny fragment of light helps us see how to make things better. You and I have a healing role in this world. It begins with light.

Illuminate the miracle of you.

During an eclipse, animals echo their chirps, calls, and howls in a false dawn chorus. Watching it unfold, whether in totality or partial blockage, is humbling and exhilarating. For a few minutes we all gather outside, sharing perspectives and protective glasses. Together, we look up with reverence and admiration. An eclipse obscures light. With a fraction of its powerful penetration, even a mere two percent of sunlight can still fill the sky so we may see. If two percent of the sun can bring light, what about two percent of me?

When I am worn out, succumbing to the heavy saturation of negativity and disbelief, I can still bring light.

You can, too.

All of me may not be where I want to be, but I can still illuminate someone else's life.

What if your thoughtful, kind reply moved apprehension to rejuvenation?

Surround yourself with people who light paths to vivacious, glorious whole living.

Live in the light.

My friend Marisa is light. She had cervical cancer and it ravaged her body with complications. Doctors could not determine the best course of treatment. She was exhausted from chemotherapy, wound care, weight loss, and wondering about survival. She fought her insurance company and doctors for a rare and promising surgery. She won.

The day before the procedure we sat at her house. Doctors warned if the cancer had spread, if there was nothing more they could do, they would sew her back up and she would go home. Marisa claimed more. So beautiful, so frail. Surrounded by a few friends, we laughed, cried, and kissed her head. Amid our hope to buoy her spirits, she spoke more light than we could ever offer.

She simply said, "I am a miracle."

Before the outcome, she knew the truth.

I am a miracle.

Do you believe this about yourself?

Not just on days of victories with crowds dancing, chanting, and cheering, but in your ordinary pace of life, do you accept this extraordinary truth?

You are a miracle.

"Nah, not me. Not now."

"I haven't …"

"I'm not …"

"It's no big deal …"

Those doubts are darkness. They are lies preventing us from becoming.

You survived childbirth. You are a miracle. There is light in you and work to do.

With light we see we don't have to wait until we become or achieve before we act. With light, we go.

Like much of what is needed for an electrifying life, we forget the source. We miss the gift of allowing light to come in and transform us. We need reminders. Marisa is now healthy, focused on raising her boys, and excelling in her career. As years go by, she may forget her brave proclamation of light. She needs a sign. I asked Hope, next door, to paint a small canvas with four words. Hope made way for light.

Marisa's sign:

I am a miracle.

She is.

I am.

You are.

Where will you put your sign?

What will you do with this truth?

Loving people and bitter people may live together in the same home, neighborhood, and nation. Same realm. Different light.

Communion begins in light and darkness. Every day is the day to heal, forgive, share empathy, and offer kindness.

There is an old story attributed to Mother Teresa, winner of the Nobel Peace Prize, a Congressional Gold Medal, and the Presidential Medal of Freedom. She worked with lonely, isolated people and described one such elderly man who had given up hope. Among discarded dishes, laundry, and darkness, she spied a beautiful, dusty, unused lamp. She offered to clean it up and light it, but the old man shrugged at the offer as no one would come to see him, and he had no need for light. (Do we ever feel this way?) She then asked if he would light the lamp each night if her sisters came to visit. He heartily agreed. And so, they visited him in the evenings, lighting the lamp and seeing each other. Mother Teresa goes on, years pass, and she forgets this man, but he remembers. Eventually, he sends a message to her assuring that the light she lit in him shines still.

Struggle is often lackluster. Light is beautiful.

You are here. You can light a dull, dusty, unused lamp. You do not have to travel the globe to bring light in darkness. Pick up the phone, text someone and tell them something they have done to light your life. You may think it is insignificant. Years pass and we forget our work and living and difference. Share light and you can change their view of all they can become with all they already are.

Do not neglect the small things.

Do not let darkness be.

You are the light that shines still.

Dad and me - two.

When Sully and I got married my dad had several roles: light-bearer, cheerleader, champion, father of the bride, and minister. His tenderness for the day inked our marriage license. As the officiate, he swore with his signature we were married on February 22, 1922.

02-22-22

In his defense, we got married at two o'clock. There were a lot of significant two's that day. When we got home from our honeymoon, I called the local clerk's office and she told me to use a sharpie for the correction. Who knew, other than a three-year-old with an uncapped color and a freshly wallpapered room, that a marker had such power? It was a small thing, easily changed and forgotten. I kept one copy with the incorrect date for posterity and a smile.

Years later, when my father was sick, I asked for a sign. We shared the same thoughts on living, dying, and death. Still, in my vulnerability of losing him and the gift of a long goodbye, I asked him if he would send me a sign. He assured me he'd have a rainbow put in the sky.

"Lame," I teased in a slow exaggeration.

"That is common, easily explained. Give me a *solid* assurance."

Dad died in the middle of a Florida hurricane. We were at home for hours with him after he took his last breath because few could reach us. We ached through the memorial service and afterwards took Mom to the beach for a few days. I walked along the shore with Sully and our boys, crying, and missing Dad's light. I looked at the water and then looked up and saw the arc.

An inverted rainbow filled the sky.

Instead of ends pointing to the ground, we could just see the curved bow with the rest of the rainbow pointing upward.

This phenomenon is called a circumzenithal arc.

As meteorologists on Weather.com explain, the phenomenon results "from the refraction of sunlight through plate-shaped ice crystals, typically forming up to a quarter-circle centered on the point in the sky directly above you." Rainbows require sunlight refracting through raindrops, whereas these arcs are formed by ice crystals high in the atmosphere, making them hard to see.

For circumzenithal arcs to form, "the sun has to be 5 to 32 degrees above the horizon. An angle of about 22 degrees above the horizon gives the optimal brightness, arc length, and width for viewing."

At *22 degrees* for optimal viewing, these arcs look like upside down rainbows, offering a broad smile in the sky.

I captured the 22-degree grin. When you enter our home, you will see the picture of Dad's arc. I went looking for a sign and found it when I looked up.

I understand if, for you, this is a coincidence or merely the circumstances of weather on a late summer day. The old idiom remains honest and accurate - beauty is in the eye of the beholder. Light is for everyone and it is also deeply personal. For me, a brief multi-colored light in the sky overcame my present darkness. It was a quiet light filling a clamoring, deep hole in my heart.

No matter our background and varied beliefs, we all find signs of light and life that bring us hope. It's the reason you can go from feeling bleak to bright as you drive in the car and hear a favorite song. Windows down, air on, pounding the wheel as you belt out the words, the light overtakes the dark.

I am thankful for light. I am humbled by its soothing shimmer and illustrious power.

Years later, we were with our kids answering questions about Dad's work in marching for the oppressed, fighting for justice and equal rights, and speaking up when it was scary and life-threatening to do so.

We reminded the kids that when things seem insurmountable, look up.

A police officer vacationing with his family noticed it first.

He said, "Would you look at that. The sun is encircled with a rainbow."

On an already beautiful day with our family laughing and racing from our favorite vacation path of pool to ocean shore, I did not expect more. There it was, another rainbow unlike any I had ever seen.

This multi-colored ring around the sun, is called a "halo" - a *22-degree halo*.

We each find light when we need it, as we need it, if we only look up.

Signs of light and life.

A sign in Sandy Springs, Georgia offers a singular statement of light: *It will be okay.*

I like this sign, but also believe it needs more.

How will it be okay? What will make it okay, even if what we hope for does not come to fruition - at all or yet.

Marriages fail. People die, it is not okay. We get through, not over. Okay happens through multiple factors and purposeful, loving choices. Okay takes time. Okay is in the eye of the beholder.

Our foyer holds the images of Dad's arc, the summer halo, and a piece of art sharing how we know things will be okay. Grit, grace, hope, and love are four primary reasons for how and why life moves from awful to okay.

Come to our house and you'll see assurances as you enter. They are small things, tiny reminders of the miracles that happen when we choose to live a whole life.

Put signs up on your walls. Put them on your doors and on your heart.

Remember.

Celebrate and sing.

The bravest thing you do is choosing to love and let light in.

People diminish light with a flick.

Want to change your whole life? Begin with believing you are beautiful. You are fallible, and yet you are loved and beautiful. Now move into the radical, hard truth that changes your whole life.

So is he.

So is she.

So are we.

This is us. We are light and love when we see the beauty, when we accept the truth.

There is beauty and blessing in brokenness.

Darkness never fully goes away, but light will always overcome if we let it in.

Your unshakable, paramount identity is accepting you are beautiful, loved, and blessed. This is who we are; what we become depends on if we plant this truth in someone else. This is a light of life.

It is easy to forget. Put up signs.

Make one, be one, for a friend.

Love your neighbor.

Be light.

Let it shine, let it shine, let it shine.

Love conquers the epidemic of empty.

CHAPTER FOURTEEN

LOVE

Open your eyes to love's miraculous capacity.

We may not share the same faith or native tongue, but we can still relate.

Let love be your strongest motivation. Choose action over announcement.

Love is our purpose.

When I was eleven, the phone rang with a soft female voice speaking on the other end. She asked if my dad was there and I said, "He and Mom are on a walk right now."

"Have him call me as soon as he gets home." These may have been her last words.

I gave Dad the message soon thereafter, but by the time he arrived at the woman's home, her husband had shot and killed her. Conviction, prison, and years later, release. Dad did not forget. He forged healing. He invited the murderer to our home for a meal. I was shocked. The essence of a prosecutor was surging in me, long before it became me. I asked, "How can you have this man over for dinner? He killed his wife. He robbed his children of a mother. He is released and should be confined."

Dad said, "Sarah girl, I am going to pray with him and love him. I am not going to excuse the harm or hurt. This is what love calls me to do."

Love is astounding and confounding.

Love is a balm healing from the inside out.

Love is.

We muck it up in attempts to marginalize and minimalize people and ideas – whether intentionally or because we have not uncovered the truth.

For hundreds of years, the portrayal of Viking warrior women fighting alongside men was considered a myth. Although depicted in art for centuries and skeletal structures in graves suggested women were battle warriors, it wasn't until recently that DNA evidence enabled scientists to prove the existence of a female Viking combatant. Our ignorance did not change their glory in battle. It happened.

Love wondrously changes life, beautifully altering our story. Quit boxing yourself into a stifled, false definition of who you are because of someone else's opinion. Don't worry about what they have yet to discover. Accept love's anthem – you are beautifully, wonderfully made. Nothing has to be perfected for love's acceptance. No one is too far from love's reach. That's a hard mantra to hold when you consider someone who perpetuates pain. It doesn't mean they live without consequences. If you are a knucklehead, you face knucklehead consequences – some immediate, some playing out over time. Life is not a continuous thread of all or nothing, win or lose extremes. Love offers meaningful growth and transformational discoveries on the horizon.

Loving now loves a generation to come.

Love conquers the epidemic of empty.

We suffer from an *epidemic of empty*. We amass things, post perfected pictures, stay busy, improve technology, buy it, and remain unfulfilled. We wonder,

How do I have all this and nothing to show for my life?

How am I twenty (or thirty, forty or sixty-five) and missing meaning?

Why am I?

Why can't I?

When will I?

Not happy, not depressed. Simply empty.

We are empty aggregators who can only be filled for a robust, exhilarating, freeing whole life by rejuvenating love.

Love revives when it is active, alive, and shared. It requires practice.

Love in action is a choice. We *choose* the acts of patience, kindness, compassion, humbleness, goodwill, and endurance. There are days it may take every molecule within us to summon the strength to love. Other moments are easy and effervescent. Each of us ought to ask ourselves a daily question: Am I strengthening and lengthening the chain of hate or will I break it?

Love doesn't fly off the handle. Love rejoices in truth and delights in bliss. Love is not idle. Love doesn't mean you put up with abuse, unfair wages or filth. Contentment is not complacency.

You can be loving in persistence and distance. Love is the strength to walk away. Love is also taking the battle to the Supreme Court or the kitchen table and seeking positive resolution. Love is calling out a wrong without casting darkness. This is best done by not beginning with the easily uttered parental or superior sentence, "What the heck is wrong with you?"

You live in your kingdom. I in mine. What an extraordinary moment when we see each other and love one another.

Labors of love.

A man without ambition is dead. A man with ambition
but not love is dead. A man with ambition and love for
his blessings here on earth is ever so alive.

- PEARL BAILEY

What does criminality look like in a modern world?

Are we willing to boldly love because it is the ethical, right, honest, decent thing to do?

Love lasts because of passion, connection, and consistency. This is true for every relationship whether at work or at home. Intimacy is far more than sex. Intimacy is a component of vulnerability. Vulnerability is a seed of love. You can be vulnerable with your clothes on. Ask anyone who is terrified to give a speech and must give one in the next ten minutes. Insecurities, fears, addictions, stress, pain, anger, guilt, and vanity are all septic suitors. We are poisoned by false measurements, mentors, and models declaring what defines prosperity and success. Loyalty, like love, is a term we muddy with our own self-interests. Loyalty does not denote competency. If I am loyal to you as friend and then lie, cheat, and steal to achieve our shared goals, morality is lost; my soul is compromised. My spirit is weakened, and my performance will never reach its wonderous potential. I will slowly lose the capacity to best weigh decisions. Loyalty can blind us from blatant corruption unless it is combined with ethics, accountability, supportive care, respect, listening, trust, empathy, integrity, and a commitment to the well-being of others. Loyalty needs love.

Love isn't just written in the stars. It is carved into the mundane, absurd, and profound. It sculpts a masterpiece from a seemingly obscure, dense, amorphous stone. In every age, love is the potent force propelling life. Love persists through relentless disappointment and despair. Love is energy. Love is the optimal recharge - minus the frustrating search for a missing power cord.

Choosing to love at home and at work isn't a trite call or trivial decision. Putting love in action leads to higher retention rates and happier employees. It's argued that we each spend more than a third of our life at work and a majority of us are unhappy with our jobs. Combine travel, overtime, and rest required for recovering from work-related fatigue and the percentage of your life spent on work increases. If you won the lottery today, would you fly out the door? The always on, 24/7 digital economy expands workdays bringing added strain on physical and mental health. People can spend decades on work they are good at, while longing for meaning, wholeness, and health. Loving homes and loving relationships encourage people to try new ventures that are scary and at the heart of their joy.

Write the book. Get fit. Learn to fly a plane. Go back to school. Switch majors. Join a choir, study or small group. Get counseling. Apply for a more senior role and seek a higher salary. Take the pay cut and teach in a prison. Be the first to do something; do it because of love.

Bosses, friends, and influencers may argue the goal is to "kick a** and take names" or "f*** s*** up." These edicts are fleeting. At best, they offer momentary medals.

Why is love so powerful?

Because it stands in sustaining, profound, and foundational contrast to every flashy, crush-someone-else-to-gain-your-fame mantra.

Love is a contributory life. You can solve the problem, win the client, close the deal, pass the test, and mend the relationship without degrading and destroying people. Love is our greatest warrior weapon; love is our sword and shield.

Love is the destination and road. It is always in us, even when we are temporarily lost.

Love doesn't take away all the hardships, difficulties, or struggles; love makes pain bearable. Love overcomes.

Most of us picture hate as looking like someone or something else, when we are all capable of holding torches to hurt and harm. We know love's absence.

Power can rest in fear.

Power can rest in love.

Love is always the far greater reward.

Love-driven leadership.

Corporations choose love by persistently empowering individuals and teams, electrifying training, serving others for a common good, fostering social events where co-workers from a cross section of divisions connect, setting clear goals and corresponding rewards, giving employees the freedom to experiment and fail, providing easy access to care and growth, offering highly competitive compensation, and elevating compassion over expediency.

Love happens in hospitals when stories of a patient's life - beyond a medical malady - are an integral part of a patient's electronic medical record. Doctors do not rush in the room for quick updates and evaluations, and instead begin with an integral picture of a life lived. Understanding a patient's passions, hopes, and journey elevates the quality of care and healing. It makes questions more relevant and with each interchange the connections and care flourish. Capturing stories honors the patient, his loved ones, and caregivers by making the healing relationship one where all are invested in passion, commitment, and consistency. Love is compassion-centered medicine.

Love at work enables an insurance company to radically increase its customer satisfaction when claims adjustors treat every call as a gift for them to help people. They are trained with techniques from counselors who understand post-traumatic stress and how any call to the insurance company may cause a client to relive a traumatic event. Love-driven organizations see the exponential value in people carrying one another. Love is thoughtfully listening to people's heartaches and dreams, helping them become whole, and guiding risk management. Doing so smartly increases satisfaction, scalability, and profits.

Love-driven leaders do five pivotal things:

1. **Recognize love is the lingering "wow."** In this age of polarizing politics and social media accelerated rage, the art of radical kindness, active listening, and empathy are revolutionary advantages. Treat everyone like beloved human beings and you

will stand out far beyond your competition. Love-driven leaders create environments where people can be who they are at home and at work with mutual respect for others. This doesn't mean I can come to work and put my stinky bare feet on the conference room table. There are consequences for reckless, egregious, or selfish decisions, including immediate termination. Goals are spelled out and lived out. Love is, "do as I do" leadership. Complaints are received with sincerity and a willingness to refine skills and solve problems.

2. **Hone humility.** Love-driven leaders speak highly of others instead of bragging about themselves. Their social media posts are filled with inspiration above self-congratulation. They are advocates who know people by name and have spent time connecting and sharing stories. Loving leaders excel because they humbly listen, express gratitude, walk with integrity, apologize, and admit mistakes while being teachable and reachable.

3. **Celebrate individuality and the team.** Love-driven leaders recognize that a team is whomever is right in front of you. Barista, board member, or baby – opportunity awaits to astoundingly alight life. Lead in love and you create environments where optimism is abundant and ideations come to life, breaking down barriers of isolation and emptiness. Leaders who love offer room for failure. Employees respect each other. There are chores, performance expectations, deadlines, shared values, frustrations, constructive remedies for conflict, and open dialogue. Teams create, innovate, pitch ideas, get turned down, and are cheered to try again. If careful craftsmanship, ingenuity, imagination, rigorous experimentation, and persistence built the rocket and

it fails to launch, the loving leader says, "Let's do it again," or "Let's do it differently using what we've learned."

4. **Embrace wholistic growth.** Loving leaders make changes meaningful, purposeful, and valuable for all impacted. They do not re-org for re-org's sake. They encourage adventure and building beyond the existing task. They stretch perceptions of what is possible, and do so with joy, not puzzling messages and droplets of doubt. Love-driven leaders inspire people to pursue passions outside of existing roles, such as training for a first triathlon or helping sex trafficking victims learn interviewing and job skills.

5. **Share the wealth.** Every engagement and interaction throughout the day is our chance to lift people up with hope, happiness, and warmth. To brighten or belittle happens in the flash of a thank you, welcome or rebuff. Life-changing love is often as easy as giving someone a few minutes of your full attention. If you ever seek feedback on how you lead with love, do something constructive with the results. People get frustrated filling out surveys and seeing things remain the same.

Be a love-driven leader. The benefits of a love-centered home, workplace, and friendship are:

- **Increasing fulfillment and meaning.**
- **Improving lives while accelerating impact, profit, and value.**
- **Furthering enduring power and influence.**
- **Expanding joy in the day-to-day.**
- **Defeating the high castle conundrum.** We often achieve power by helping people, and then have a propensity to let

the role distort and destroy the good that got us there. Others watch, sigh, and perhaps grumble, "She was so great until she got the new role and became a jerk." We are all susceptible to abusing power and treating people poorly for our own gain. Love-centered leaders are not selfish or rude. They are not greedy or arrogant. They adapt, communicate well and often, dignify people with kindness, share joy, and instill calm amidst the storms. They labor with love.

Let love linger.

My girlfriends and I entered a restaurant for an early lunch. Huge bouquets of roses filled every corner and counter. Our table wasn't ready, and a waiter asked if we'd care to wait with a glass of champagne. It was vacation. We immediately said, "Yes." Only a few sips separated us, and we were seated outside on a gorgeous sunny day. With the ideal temperature and company, we lingered, lost in conversation and laughter. We were on a girls' weekend and had already logged hours in serious, dynamic, and delicious discussions. There was more to say. For three hours we stayed at the table, never rushed or checking the time – we were lost and found, lingering in love. When we paid the bill, and decided it was time to go, a waiter came and filled our glasses. I thanked him for his thoughtfulness and said, "I know you need to turn these tables and I'm sorry we stayed so long. I can't believe you're pouring more, as if encouraging us to stay."

He said, "I am. Go ahead and linger."

Linger a little longer in love.

Stay a little longer in bed alone or with your beloved, the kids, the dog, or all. Stay a little longer at the office when work is invigorating, inspiring, and engaging. Stay a little longer on a friend's couch or at the dinner table. Stay a little longer in hilarious, loving text string.

Stay a little longer on the field, watching kids play catch after practice is over. When it's time to go, open your arms again and earnestly say, "I love watching you play!" They need to hear this more than any critique or hopes for a college career. You need to hear this truth and call from love.

I love you.

I love watching you play.

Linger here.

Love cautions: Beware of the monkey menace.

We are planning a trip to Kenya. Our preparation includes written warnings and a correlating picture of a cautionary message hanging inside our accommodations:

WHEN LEAVING THE ROOM, REMEMBER TO CLOSE WINDOWS BECAUSE OF MONKEY MENACE.

The monkeys will take anything and everything and leave behind things you do not want to receive. Cough medicine, jewelry, coins are all up for grabs. If you want to keep your room intact, do not open doors or windows for monkeys. We need this warning. Do not let monkeys pierce your beautiful heart. Love one another. Take care. Beware of monkey menace.

Quit arguing with naysayers. Stop listening to hateful lies and destruction. Pursue your joys. Ever find yourself fixing problems and filling other people's holes while neglecting what you are called to do? Leave any crazy making monkeys outside. You can love them with respect, honoring where they are and where you need to be without making yourself vulnerable to their messes.

I'm arguably being a bit harsh on equating *all* monkeys with menace. I'm convicted by my own admonition after seeing this headline: *Hero Monkey Helped Lost Man Survive for Days In The Amazon.*
There are monkey outliers. Some throw feces. Some throw fruit.
Beware of where you walk and what you take in.

Behold, love.

"Behold!" is an introduction to a wondrous sight. When our daughter, Cecily, was two, she claimed this word and used it to declare acts of valor, mystery, and two-year-oldness.

Entire economy-sized bag of carrots spilled on the floor, "Behold!"
Tower of blocks, modelling clay, and paint intertwined, "Behold!"
Creating a toilet paper bridge from her room to the inside of an overflowing toilet, "Behold!"

Maybe we seldom write, sing, or declare "Behold!" because we understand it ushers in magnificent love. Maybe we are not willing to see or believe all such love will bring. Behold offers the awesome and overwhelming. Wondrous love overwhelms as we are not fully sure what to do with this gift. Immaturity and insecurity block love's bloom. Eight-year-olds are often better at boldly accepting and sharing love than adults. Let's face it, loving people is difficult. Raining rancor is fun, particularly as others pile on. Justification and indignation override guilt and level-headed decisions. It's easier to annihilate and apologize later or never. We fail to guide and guard our hearts. We look for easier routes, opting to stay in trenches rather than forging to battle. Love is not the work of wimps.

We may wonder,

"How can I possibly do what is required?"

"It's impossible. It's impassable."

"No one would listen to me."

"I don't know how."

"I don't know where to begin."

The answer:

Behold, **Love.**

This is you. Love is your name.

Behold, **love.**

Love is your challenge, comfort, and charge.

Love comes running.

Our daughter Gabrielle made a card for her teacher. She did so in the honest, carefree way children make things for someone they love. She comprised a test with twenty-six options, descriptors the test taker could choose to describe himself. A wrinkled white paper, drawn on by red pen, oversized circles - not all fully enclosed, misspellings – coura- giouse, awsum – it was perfect. This little girl reached her twenty-fifth option and wrote, *loved by me.* The last choice on the list of praises was "all of the above." Gabrielle took the test, filling in the final option and went to find her teacher. But she missed him and gave the sheet to another instructor.

Would he see it?

Do tiny acts of love matter?

They do. They always have.

Pieces of love are what pull us together to become all we are called to be.

This beloved, longtime, trusted family friend offered one of his own.

It said –

Dear Gabrielle,

Thank you so much for the sweet note. It made my day. I hope you know I do love you and can't wait to watch all the great things you will do.

Gabrielle, you have been blessed with a wonderful family, a beautiful personality, and a gifted mind. You can and will do great things.

If I can ever help you or your family in any way, just call.

I will drop everything and come to you.

People can go a lifetime without ever getting a note, a promise, and follow through of love.

His words rest on Gabrielle's dresser and remain in our hearts.

Who will you drop everything for and come running?

Do they know?

Do you?

An astonishing, incredible whole life is one where we have relationships compelling us to run to each other.

Maybe you once were willing to run and hurt got in the way. If you will run today, tell them. One of the biggest regrets people have at the end of their life is not telling people how much they love them.

If you'll come running, you love.

Our daughter Cecily got a similar letter from her third-grade teacher, Miss Hilary. It came like an offering to hold her hand with assurance. One morning Cecily woke tired and worried about a test. She studied the night before and rose early to study more. I placed Hilary's note on top of her book bag and went into the kitchen to make coffee. A few moments later, Cecily came into the kitchen and said, of Hilary, "I love her so much. I can't believe how much she loves me. She is always beautiful."

Yes, Cecily, she is.

So are you.

You, my friend, are loved and lovely. You are beautiful.

Let love drive your decisions when what you want to do and what you should do are far afield.

Let love define and refine, soften, and sharpen.

Our whole life is our reply to love.

When she was 75 years old, Maya Angelou sat down for a poignant interview with Lucinda Moore of *Smithsonian Magazine*. Published in April 2003, Ms. Angelou shared two moments of profound liberation, both occurring in her early twenties. The first was realizing she could die. Initially it was scary, but then accepting her mortality empowered her to choose to fully enjoy life. The second liberation came during a walk with her mother. Grit, grace, hope, and love brought her home.

She shared,

> "I had two jobs. I was raising my son. We had a tiny little place to live. My mother had a 14-room house and someone to look after things. She owned a hotel, lots of

diamonds. I wouldn't accept anything from her. But once a month she'd cook for me. And I would go to her house and she'd be dressed beautifully.

One day after we'd had lunch, she had to go somewhere. She put on silver-fox furs—this was when the head of one fox would seem to bite into the head of the other—and she would wear them with the tails in front; she would turn it around with the furs arching back. We were halfway down the hill and she said, 'Baby'—and she was small; she was 5- feet-4 1/2 and I'm 6 foot—'You know something? I think you're the greatest woman I've ever met.' We stopped. I looked down at this pretty little woman made up so perfectly, diamonds in her ears. She said, 'Mary McLeod Bethune, Eleanor Roosevelt, my mother and you—you are the greatest.' It still brings me to te——.

[Her eyes tear up.]

We walked down to the bottom of the hill. She crossed the street to the right to get into her car. I continued across the street and waited for the streetcar. And I got onto the streetcar and I walked to the back. I shall never forget it. I remember the wooden planks of the streetcar. The way the light came through the window. And I thought, suppose she's right? She's very intelligent, and she's too mean to lie.

Suppose I really am somebody?

Those two incidents liberated me to think large thoughts, whether I could comprehend them or not [she laughs], but to think ...."

Suppose you really are somebody?

Love says you are.

What is your reply?

Let love light and liberate your whole life.

CHAPTER FIFTEEN

BUILD YOUR BRIDGE

Bridge building is always an epic tale.

Dr. Martin Luther King, Jr. delivered sermons not far from where I sit today. He spoke, and all would behold. He told of dreams, mercy, standing up, and working together. He dared to love.

How do we love all *and* solve the problems of the world?

How do we love amidst the chasms dividing us by race, gender, political party, faith, and social status?

We build bridges.

Love calls.

The courageous reply: build your bridge.

We are here because of bridges we build and bridges we cross.

My parents fought for civil rights and equality for all, and I still had to clean the bathroom each week, while my younger brother took out the trash. I like to tease Mom about those gender specific chores mandated by a couple who said we all have limitless potential.

When my mom and dad fell in love, he was the top salesman for Yardley of London. She worked at U.S. Steel. She thought their life would be fully secure, and then as a couple they gave it all away to start over and serve. It was hard, wonderful, scary, lonely, and captivating. Living on Emory University's campus at the height of the Civil Rights movement and the assassination of Dr. Martin Luther King, Jr., my parents built bridges through service and love. Dad saw pain and opposition between people as an opportunity to heal and bond. He had no skills in ironwork or casting concrete beams, but knew how to bring people together to listen, strengthen, and renew. He spoke ideas and dreams of equality in the face of racists and cynics, and he persevered. He invited people in and offered them a seat and a voice at the table.

When Dr. King died, Atlanta was filled with pain, chaos, and confusion. Mourners descended on an aching, divided city. In the rift of hurt, people built bridges. My parents opened their tiny home to strangers, picked people up from the airport, served meals, stood together with those of different backgrounds and faiths, walked in the funeral procession, and helped grieving souls carry each other. They rallied, not knowing precisely how to build their bridges. They just built them in small beautiful ways with stones of hope, beams of kindness, and bonds of love. My mom maintains their life's work began with death.

Life springing forth in death - this is love.

Time and technology advance and yet, we still face tragedies, uncertainty, injustice, and storms of doubt.

We can build bridges. You and me. We are bridge builders when we choose to love.

We don't need to become something before we build something.

You are able, as you are, to build your bridge.

In Atlanta, we live amongst the iconic. We may feel far from becoming legendary, but each of us has the power to leave a legacy of love. Every day we can tame and make gentle the world by building bridges.

Civil rights leader and broadcasting executive Xernona Clayton lived in Atlanta in the 1960s and was appointed to oversee a neighborhood improvement program. She knew Dr. King and was a good friend to his wife, Coretta Scott King. One of Ms. Clayton's neighborhood captains was a grand dragon in the Ku Klux Klan. Terrifying, troubling opposition. Eventually they began talking and built a bridge. They didn't agree, but he enjoyed meeting with her, and they listened to each other.

Then one day in 1968, this leader of an oppressive and evil faction, renounced his membership in the KKK and proclaimed he would dedicate his life to uniting people instead of dividing.

Bridge building begins within. It takes time. Transformation requires contemplation. A durable bridge is built in a layer upon layer, conversation by conversation process. The victories are intermittent and progress plodding. Unevenly distributed weight from compounding and compressing stress can lead to fractures and potentially further the divide.

If bridging gaps requires such hard, time-consuming labor, why do it? After all, you may attempt to build a bridge and discover it is a painful one-way crossing. And what if I build a bridge, but I never cross it? History is filled with those who press on and never cross the bridge of their design. Blowing-up bridges in wartime is a way to protect your army from an oncoming enemy, so how do we know when to build or blow?

Attitude has the greatest impact. If the work makes you come alive, you build on. Sometimes it feels like we are clawing our way through a tight tunnel instead of constructing a wide, arched pathway. Battered and bruised, we find light and connection in our exhaustion. Rest comes when we find others who will take up the hoisting helm. We all face common joys and trials and may remain mysteries to each other. We are adversaries of the unfamiliar. We face a constant low hum of hurt, stereotypes, and self-doubt. The difference between a hostile, bitter existence and a loving whole life? A sturdy bridge.

Breaking out of systemic toxic cycles requires a link of love. If a child, teen, or adult has one person who consistently believes in them, who sees them, who has ideas for overwhelming questions like, "Now what?" and predicts needs before they arise, they are exponentially more likely to thrive. Fellowship is freedom work, releasing the aches of a stained soul. We root for each other. We survive through community.

Community begins with a bridge.

Community is a shared public spirit, a union with common ownership in purpose, values, and fellowship. A beautiful, echoing *communion* magnifies with rituals of welcome, aid, compassion, and a mutual meaningful cause. Rituals rejuvenate teams, families, and neighborhoods.

Here are three powerful rituals for raising whole communities:

1. **Practice persistent welcome.** When a new neighbor moves in next door, bring them bread, share your contact information, and follow-up with periodic welcoming assurance. When someone is released from prison, whether a barbed wire barri-

cade *or a self-made tomb*, welcome them back into community. This is needed for people who were incarcerated *or alienated* because of bad choices or circumstances (crimes, marital affairs, financial ruin, and addiction.) We expend vast energy and capital on punishment and run from the complexities in the return to community. Most captives are released. Rituals of hospitality reduce recidivism and help multiple generations, whether through job interviews, counseling or barbeques. We don't celebrate the harm and hurt; we ready people for a path of hope and purpose. We bravely love by honoring and supporting victims while huddling in the hard work of restoration. This begins with remembering someone's name and pain. Connection is sustenance. We are wired for welcome.

2. **Show up for Sunday night supper**. Regularly meet with friends, family, and a stranger or two for a bigger purpose, at a fixed time, with phones off. Any night will do. Nourish spirits, enrich minds, and recognize souls are unbound by age, color, or status.

3. **Commit to love.** If you know an easier way, share it. Help people with transitions. Going from pre-k to kindergarten is scary. Heading from a hospital to a rehab facility is rough. Comfort comes through the wisdom of those who have gone before us. Life is a common joy and struggle. Share the load with love.

Giving the middle finger may seem like a better option but consider the ultimate outcome. What will bring the change we seek? Admittedly this is a tough call when driving. Why don't you let me merge? Why are you suddenly defensive upon seeing my blinker? Why won't you use a blinker? Some questions have no answers. Like when a bumper sticker exerts one belief and driving gestures convey another.

We persevere with grit, grace, hope *and love.*

And love is not just the conclusion of four pillars. It signifies setting apart what binds everything else – LOVE.

In a local elementary school, there is a quote of connection painted on the wall encouraging kids to be kind. The advice offered is that even though others might be smarter or more athletic, you should choose to be kind. It's a good message, however it lacks the essential - *why.* Why be kind? What will it bring? How will it sculpt a dream or right an injustice? For our whole lives, love is the why.

My dad was once assigned to a fledgling church where people were in an uproar about a brick bell tower. The expense, feuding sides, and sneers brought on by the erection of the bell tower nearly broke the church. When Dad arrived the bell tower was up, attendance was low, and tensions were high. The congregation needed a bridge. Dad began by bringing people in to ring the bell for joys. Community members of all faiths were welcome. When couples got married, they shared a kiss and then a new tradition of ringing the bell together. Love turned a clanging gong into a reverberation of joy.

Rituals help fuse our physical, spiritual, and political disconnect. Establish rituals of love and you will build lasting bridges.

Love is vital for the survival of every village.

Strengthen love, identity, and belonging.

Unhappy with where you are? Build a bridge. Build them for moments and millenniums. Build them in hurts and hurrahs. Choose love, not because the other person is loving and kind, but because you are.

Forge ahead and know it is okay to stop and begin in a new way or through a new means or with an entirely new link.

Bridge building allows for ample space between both sides, an easily accessible crossing, and a place to meet in the middle. Wondering how to remedy a deepening divide? Build a bridge for her, for him, for them. Caring for other people is where our bridges begin.

We can scream and shout at the injustice or we can build bridges through education, reformation, and advocacy. We can build bridges for success with stones of hope, beams of kindness, and bonds of love.

It's not easy. It is not comfortable or immediately certain and gratifying. Life itself is a lumpy passage.

You have to consider: *What's the goal?*

To get to the other side? To protect and defend? To empower relationships and reconciliation? To pave a way for others?

Who do I want to be?

I can't be a jerk and build a lasting bridge of love.

I can attain status and stature, but I will not become all I am called to be until I build bridges with love.

Hope, kindness, and love seem far afield from work, politics or posts. Yet they yield the most growth and lasting success. Stones of hope are needed when doubt seeps in. Beams of kindness offer strength and require active listening for full support. Bonds of love help bind wounds - the ones we see and the deeper, unseen lingering pains of anguish and trauma. Love is what helps us choose collaboration instead of competition. Love is what empowers us to celebrate others' wins and offer comfort during losses. Love is the five second delay preventing us from blasting out to hurt in lieu of choosing to heal.

We are different.

There are bridges you are called to build, some girded by steel beams and covered with concrete paths and others linked by love's wings carrying ashes from a threshold of pain to a lifetime of purpose.

The bridge may begin as a simple ladder where hope is hoisted or as a small hand clasping yours before crossing a street and breaking down a bully's barrier.

There are stars only you can see.

Build them. Call them. Light them.

Lead with love.

Know your bridge takes time and is worth the work and wait, for you are worthy and worth the weight—the time, burden, and joys.

Construct your bridges even when whispers of doubt fill your head and heart.

Your bridge awaits. Let grit, grace, hope, and love build it.

Then we can beautifully walk each other home.

CHAPTER SIXTEEN

SHUSH

The top left half of my PC screen is shattered. Captivating cracks led me to absentmindedly swipe my index finger across the damage, allowing tiny shards to pierce and sting. The device slipped from overloaded arms unpacking the car. Easily done when trying to get six people shuffled from a stuffed animal strewn, pillow filled, luggage laden SUV. It didn't seem like an ominous or far fall to the ground. I couldn't see any damage until I opened it up.

My finger bled while I tried to remove the glass, avoiding dripping blood on the unsullied white hotel room bedding. In my frustration, my family rallied. One dug in a Dopp kit searching for a bandage. Another said he heard of a guy who fixes glass screens. All expressed their sorrow assuring everything will be okay. Our youngest, Gabrielle, looked at the damaged corner which vacillated from a disco ball effect to crushed ice radiating lines on a snowy day and happily exclaimed, "The brokenness looks so cool!"

While I'm wondering if any of my work is lost and if I'll have to buy a new PC, she holds a much different perspective.

She discovers beauty.

She clings to what is good.

How will I reply?

Are we quick to welcome unexpected optimism? Or do we flick it away, feeling such idealism is inauthentic and unhelpful? Do our words hit back or love back?

The person we are in conversation with most is ourselves. Our inner narration provides justification for right and wrong answers. The distinction rests with our focus, faith, and dependence. What we say to ourselves shapes where we go and what we become. Our inner-critic pummels in shadows with lies appearing as truths. We belong to the day. We are all day people, given the chance to bathe in the same light. We do not belong to darkness, but often find ourselves lingering there without armor. One word is the best shield:

"Shush."

This is the quiet bringing beauty from ashes.

Your mind is holy ground. Be careful what treads and threads. Anxiety, stress, insecurity, and deception scheme. They gain strength with exhaustion, and just when you think you're plowing along, these agitating agents throttle you with a low self-worth wallop. Everyone is susceptible to an illogical interruption. Whole life warriors consistently combat and overcome the negative self-talk.

It takes practice. Suffering in noise no one else hears, you think you are alone, but you are not. Trouble is a crooked, feisty, persistent creature. Our bodies crave rest. Distress slithers from our consistency on phones and persistently churning minds. Each require our decision to turn down the volume. Shut it completely off.

Some try to hide their overwrought, racing, worried mind with a flimsy buffer of over-confidence. They talk loudly and text quickly to silence others.

The nullifying noise in our heads can range from an occasional occurrence to overwhelming our lives.

These are long pains requiring a short reply.

Shhhh.

Hush now.

It's all right.

Shush is not a rude hand in your face or a person admonishing you in an imposing library to be quiet. It is the "shhhh" offered by a loving mother, stroking her child's head, assuring all will be okay. It is the reminder we are enough. We can do this.

Gates of hell are not ornate iron bars. They are anything separating us from the bonds of love. Division outside and inside us thwarting wholeness is defied with a solid exclamation. *Shush* is how we storm the gates—renewing and restoring ourselves. The way you bring heaven on earth is to love. Getting nonsense and destructive noise out of your head is vital to self-love.

Shush is a super shield.

Chris Evans marvels as an onscreen hero. One of his most well-known characters is a puny young man who transforms physically, gaining enormous strength and power. Grit and gumption were his skills at the onset. Evans was offered this role of the mighty, earth-saving decision-maker and found himself second guessing critical decisions in real life.

One movie seemed doable, but Evans realized saying, "yes" to a super hero gig likely meant agreeing to multi-year contracts, action figures, aggressive fans, and radical changes in life. His "yes" would alter many other lives and he knew he couldn't easily back out if things became difficult.

He sought advice. Through therapy he learned to process his pain, plug the inner noise, and calm anxiety with the shift of one word - "Shush."

In his interview with *Motivation Madness*, Evans explained the power in this word and how he uses it to rise above the noise.

It's not saying, "No."

It might mean, "Not yet."

It may even be, "Yes, of course, let's do this."

Release yourself from hours of struggling with deafening and defeating noise.

With a shush, you might discover as Chris Evans did, that maybe the thing you're most scared of is exactly what you should do.

When you silence, you soar.

Aware. Arm. Anew.

Not all inner monologue is bad. Intuition is an excellent gut check. Grounded and founded positivity, recognizing the need for forgiveness or an apology, and rethinking strategy for improving communication and whole living are all internal chatter that matters. When the self-talk becomes debilitating, when it prevents you from walking into your dreams, when worry weighs on your heart and head to the point where you focus on little else, it is time to bash the babble.

Here are three ways to get the job done: *Aware. Arm. Anew.*

1. Aware.

Decipher what is real versus what is nonsense. Where is this coming from? What do I fear? Are these thoughts helpful? Am I tired, hungry, hurt? Did I go back home for three days and revert to old, bad habits? Is this a present pain or bundled baggage from long ago? Is there a pattern and practice in me where I self-sabotage dreams? Am I embarrassed of potentially failing? Did I have a great time being at a party and then stayed awake all night ruminating about what I said or what he said or what we didn't say? Am I worried about paying a bill or is it a bigger, broader issue? Through mindfulness, prayer, a walk to clear my mind, and a conversation with a trusted counselor or friend, do I have clarity or is my head still muddied with anxiety? Why is it bothering me?

Silencing interrupting thoughts takes time and hard work. It begins with a "shush" and requires more; for if we breathe, we are thinking, beating, and repeating.

Evaluate:

Did I really screw up or am I overthinking?

Get to the root of the issue by becoming aware of the who, what, why, and how of the noise. You do not have to do so on your own.

2. Arm.

We hunger for wholeness. We lose our way before knowing we're lost. We're free while still perceiving we're blocked and barricaded.

To wholly be is not a bated breath existence. I think of our dogs staring out the window and then running to us with excited alerts for all that stirs in the world. They prance and tip tap on the floors until we open the door and expect them to dash out after their desires, and on most days they do. However, there are times we open the door and they stay. No interest in the pursuit.

It's okay to be cautious before facing a challenge. Noble warriors go to battle and triumph with trembling hands. It may look like others are soaring with ease when their wings are propelled by countless hands and headstrong hope.

In the hunt for answers and ease, embrace joy. Choose this day to ignite your whole life. Don't wait for better, cooler, simpler, or less harried and hurried. Happiness sparks in complications and calm.

People offer us portions of light and darkness. Both fuel all we become. It's an astounding gift to wield the power of choosing what you will do with your beautiful, bewildering whole life. We let moments and months go by, forgetting this bastion rests within us. *We get to choose our reply* - to exhaling breath, confounding grace, and unfailing love.

Take your whole life and this vast world into your arms. Take it in like you are savoring a sneeze-free lilac bouquet. Walk beside bliss and sorrow.

There may be things you cherish and long for that you cannot reach. Strive anyway.

Be aware of your stamina and strength. You may run around believing you are saving everyone while treading water and miss that you are drowning.

There are people who take the broken pieces of life and make mosaics. Cling to them. Be them. Share the art.

Accept that no matter how nice, talented, or generous you are, there will be people who do not like you. Make sure the enemy does not reside within. The greatest infirmity is to destroy yourself from the inside out.

You are not meant for a life of timidity. You may think you are holding on to the guard rail with a weak and worn wrist, when the truth is you are holding up the universe.

It is time to boldly live in your wholeness. Find your heaven here.

3. Anew.

Restoration arises in a good night's sleep and in painstakingly detailed renovation. Life's blows come in waves and it is critical to learn how to steady yourself or plug your nose. I recently took a flight for work and as the captain turned off the fasten seatbelt sign, the woman next to me opened a can of tuna to eat for lunch. The guy behind me had just finished two hot dogs loaded with relish and sauerkraut. These distinctive aromas wafted as I wallowed in the tedious two-hour flight. While I'd love a moratorium on allowing such items in cramped spaces with windows I cannot open, I must decide how I will let irritants impact me. I am the master of my reply. Because it's not just fragrant food or smelly feet on the plane, it's the complex client issue waiting as I disembark, it's the stress in my house as I worry over something the kids are facing and medical care for aging parents and unfilled dreams I let float further away as I see life whirling at warp speed. Then I catch myself in the mirror or in an inadvertent flip to selfie mode to take a picture and grimace at the sight. I don't see love's view. I sigh and wonder, "Is it too late to start anew?" This is the reality at 40,000 feet with empty tuna fish cans, bared hairy feet, and post-hot dog burps.

Roman philosopher Seneca wrote, *On The Shortness of Life*, nearly two thousand years ago. In his wisdom, he argues life is not short; we simply waste a lot of time. With a future of uncertainty, Seneca calls us to *live immediately*. There is a poignant distinction between living long versus existing long. Vibrant living is not constrained by age or condition. It is a mental ignition.

Part of the delay in living wholly is sitting with a clenched expectation of waiting for someone to do the right thing. Families find this stress when a parent dies and they hope for healing in words and disbursement of things. Don't sit in expectation for tomorrow when restoration awaits in today. Devote yourself to grit, grace, hope, and love. Stress leads to metabolic changes, including increased fatigue and burden on your body. Release the aches.

Stop wishing and start living.

Choose joy. Love more. Live as if your soul has discovered fire.

Begin with renewal through self-care. Fill yourself. Give yourself a life lift. Have the courage to honor who you are—your gifts, personality, beginnings, design, greatness within, and greatness beyond. Love your whole self before you exhaustively give away precious parts. Be the surgeon of your soul by making yourself whole. Quench the fires within so you can battle the blazes of the world. Live well in the context of imperfection. Throw off blankets of despair. This is not an investment in arrogance or narcissism. It is not permission to hurl insults or offer cruelty disguised as courage. This is blessed assurance in your whole, authentic, beautiful self so that you may bless others.

Repeat this mantra and mission: Grace. Grace. Grace.

Sleep with the strength of hope and love on your lips.

Evidence of a pattern and practice.

On my sixteenth birthday I excitedly headed off with my dad to the Division of Motor Vehicles (DMV) to take my driver's exam. I asked if we could pull over into a nearby neighborhood so I could practice parallel parking and my three-point turn one more time. Dad readily obliged. With my pre-test fervor, I hit the curb and popped the front passenger tire.

Dad didn't get angry.

He didn't yell or fuss about my mistake.

He smiled and said, "Pull over, Sarah girl. Today you're going to learn how to change a tire and get your license."

He sat on the curb and talked me through the process.

He didn't change.

I did.

His calm, his love was my "shush."

I'm loved.
I'm me.

Three of our four children are frequently asked about their heritage. Children of close friends, family members, and strangers ask,

"What are you?"

Recently, one middle-schooler inquired, "Is your grandmother black?"

I'd like to say the question was asked with light and joy for the possibility. It sadly wasn't. Middle school is deemed an isolating, singular time in life, but if we examine ourselves, we find each of us spend portions of life reiterating middle school milieu.

One day, my darker complexioned three were out selling discount coupon cards for our local high school. We have lived in our community for fifteen years. Our youngest was eight, donned in dinosaur knee socks, purple patterned shorts, and a pink t-shirt emblazoned with a sparkling heart. She begged her siblings to let her try going to the door by herself. They agreed. She skipped down the driveway, braided pig tails swaying. Somehow her presence scared someone.

The neighbor called the police. On the streets where she rides her bike, cuddles animals, throws water balloons, and courageously, freely lives, someone missed who she was and thought she was someone or something else. They forgot about the beautiful inside—the beauty in themselves and in her.

The policeman arrived. Stopped the kids. My youngest shook. Scared, trembling, tearful. The older ones, a teen and barely teen, listened, explained, and answered questions. Once the officer determined what had happened, he felt so bad. He loved on them. Encouraged them. He even bought a card. He told them not to worry.

Thank you for those who protect and parent when we are not around.

The kids came home with the story.

I had to decide.

Who I am going to be?

Will I try to love, anyway?

Will I be enraged?

Could both collide?

What will change the world to better all of us?

Who do I authentically want to be? I need to consider this question and my answer before tremendous and tough things happen.

Immediate is easy. Long term is a better and harder investment.

I gathered my circle of support.

When our children are asked, "What are you?" we talk about how they want to respond.

I remind them of all they wonderfully are.

Love is. Love remains.

And then I give them a joyful, glorious, bountiful reply.

It is true for all of us.

When asked, "What are you?"

Say,

"I'm me."

For their whole lives, for yours and mine, this is a superb, holy, and ideal place to be.

CHAPTER SEVENTEEN

THANK YOU FOR BEING

They longed for children. High school sweethearts, beautiful, married a decade, stunning in work, style, and grace. They are both artists and entrepreneurs, skilled athletes, renaissance renovators, and creative designers who bring vision, laughter, and uptick to all around them. Friends cheered for their positive pregnancy test. Ached when they did not carry to term.

People looking for definitions or explanations are often inadvertently clumsy in their attempts to comfort after a baby carried far along into the second trimester dies and the mom nearly bleeds to death. Multiple miscarriages followed. The loss, anguish, and fatigue of crushed dreams lumbered deep in Mark and Cinda for years, and still, they held hope. They persisted in prayer and innovation. Then along came baby Belle.

We shared in the joys of showers awaiting her arrival, and in the excitement of her birth, I found myself looking for a way to somehow convey my awe.

To hold her was to cradle light. There I'd stand on holy ground.

How could I capture this joy?

Four words delivered the reverberations of my grateful soul:

Thank you for being.

I shared the same maxim when her brother Rex arrived.

Now it is my favorite expression to give for any occasion.

Too often we wait for the big things to express great love.

Every day, your presence calls for someone to convey:

Thank you for being.

This truth is not contingent on a change in weight, locale or increased social media presence. There is a distinctive, unequalled calling within. Bring it to light. Figure out why and when you stopped working hard on what you love. Find ways to take your talents and serve others. Look in the mirror. Love yourself. Walk into a room knowing you belong. Stop waiting for permission to start your whole life. Act on the belief that you are wholly loved - as you are.

Typical doesn't transform. *Special* changes kings and prisoners, one conversation at a time.

You are indispensably needed for this life—the party, the dance, the clean-up, the embrace, and the rest. And you have the gift of acknowledging this in someone else.

Apparently, we need more tambourines.

We headed to Florida for a family bridal shower. My girls and I flew down on Saturday morning and our quick return flight meant we had to leave Grandma's house on Sunday at 4:45 am. I set my alarm for 4:30 and told the girls to sleep in something they could wear on the plane.

I wanted to quietly dart out, having said "goodbyes" the night before, but moms tend to mother, no matter our age and stage. At 4:20, I heard my old name,

"Sarah girl, are you up?"

She offered breakfast. We hugged, and she stood on the front walk, watching us get into the car.

I opened the passenger door and our driver, Pradeep, moved two items from the seat so I could sit down. One was a note pad, the other a tambourine. This was not just a standard circular tambourine. This was an electric-youth-blue half circle tambourine with a handgrip for jamming with a band or serious karaoke. I was thinking about this instrument's prominence as we pulled out of the driveway with my mom still watching from the front walk. She finds herself tending to her baby as I tend to mine. We give our secret family wave.

Do you have one? You should. They are fun and functional.

The wave comes in handy when a child is on stage and wants to cleverly, casually let you know they see you and you see them. Sully would give our family wave to my dad in the middle of sermons and dad would reply without skipping pastoral inspiration. A secret knowing, a loving connection, offers assurance when nerves are high or goodbyes are nigh.

Some of the smallest things we share are precious, grand acts of love.

As Mom and I get older, I get more tender about departing, but admittedly in this early hour my sight quickly turns from her to the double row metal jingles.

I placed the girls safely in the backseat with our bags. I was worried if I put the bags in the trunk, I might forget them in my exhaustion. Pradeep and I shared the front row and pleasantries.

Soon enough he turned on the radio. He picked a narrow genre—yacht rock love songs.

Kenny Rogers played, and Pradeep began to sing. He had trouble finding the notes, going too low or too high, but finally found his sweet spot just below pitch. The next song came on and as the chorus began Pradeep asked, "You know what I love to do?"

"What's that?" I replied with interest and perhaps a tiny bit of concern given the hour and his excitement.

"Just listen."

"Do you feel it?"

"When a song like this comes on, you just can't help . . ."

And then he yanked out his tambourine and shook it with vigor as his chin pulsed with a robust rhythm.

He smiled. With light in his eyes, he came alive.

Each song needed more tambourine.

And Pradeep's voice.

And affirming nods.

I was trying to process the yacht rock, love song induced tambourine joy at such a dark, early hour, when a little hand reached up from the right side of my seat. It wanted to be held. My daughter Cecily's grasp conveyed her worry, wonder, and a tad bit of laughter for what in the world was going on.

Pradeep is happy and harmless.

I realized we will likely never see him again.

I could sit, ignoring his zeal for percussion and The Doobie Brothers.

Or I could honor him and join in the humanness.

The outstretched little hand holding mine affirmed it was all initially odd and surprising, but my reaction could change the impact on

Pradeep and my daughters.

At first, I tapped a little bit, lightly drumming my fingertips on my thigh. I figured this was the least I could do. Besides, drivers rate passengers. I didn't want a poor review.

I sat there wondering what the conversation might be if Pradeep and I were to ever meet again, long past this interesting car ride.

I see who he is—content in his joy, appreciating the gifts of music. Who will I be?

Stifled? Erudite? Arrogant? Uptight?

Or would I choose to merely be in the joy of being.

The next song determined my reply.

The familiar notes, rising and readying.

A 1970s classic commands a sing-along, and unbeknownst to me, a tambourine.

We sang.

The girls shouted sweet echoes from the refrain.

Our outlook for an early morning flight changed because of a kind, happy man and his tambourine.

Pradeep, thank you for being.

Wednesday Girls.

My mom has a group of best friends. They call themselves, "The Wednesday Girls" because of the day of their weekly meeting date. Many decades have passed since their first convening where they solve problems on global, local, and personal scales. A fellow Wednesday daughter and I marvel at what these women accomplish, and yet we shouldn't, for circles of women have been changing the world since the world began.

At one meeting they asked each other about things they wish they hadn't said to their kids.

One shared the phrase she'd like to take back, "Don't get blood on the carpet!"

I understood this regretful introspection of what we utter in moments of panic, as oozing, non-life-threatening wounds rush to rest on freshly cleaned carpet or couches. My own admonishment of late becomes a plea, a gentle whisper of love, or blatant consternation depending on the moment and what job needs to be done:

"I have eighteen months to make you into a man!"

Am I repeating this for him or for me?

In this exciting time of transition, uncertainty, and pressure, what he needs to hear is:

"Jack, thank you for being."

For all four of our kids, no matter our shape and state, my overwhelming call of love is:

Thank you for being.

But I don't say it as often as I should, and I don't think of it when twenty-seven mint wrappers are stashed underneath chair cushions or it's time to leave the house and the idea of wearing shoes has suddenly slipped everyone's mind.

The Wednesday Girls encircle each other, like momma elephants protecting the herd. They rally for each other.

When you love, you rally.

We recently went to a famous amusement park in Orlando, Florida. As we walked between attractions, I glistened with sweat and nausea, realizing my body was no longer meant to do 4D rides and roller coasters without medical assistance. The wind whipped around us for a moment, sweeping a particle into our daughter Cecily's eye. Oh, it hurt! She moved her eyelid and I caught a glimpse of a small, clear piece poking out. We encircled her, offering comfort and ideas. We flushed her eye with water, had her pull her upper eyelid over the lower lid. The speck wouldn't come out. Sully looked for an employee who might guide us to a nearby nurse's station. It was way across the park. We circled Cecily for the walk. We rallied.

She was strong, but started to cry, and apologize. We shored her up and let her know the six of us were in this together. No apologies needed.

Henry and Gabrielle led. Sully and I each held a hand and Jack took the rear offering encouragement and gentle pats on her back. Along the way, the piece worked itself out of our daughter's reddened eye. The family circle cheered and together we braved the next ride.

And so, the rally goes on.

Where we danced.

Fear and doubt separate you from the abundant whole life you are called to live; love unites you with your life. Uniting begins with a whole and holistic approach to thanks and giving.

There is a special corner in our house. I remind Henry, "That's where we danced."

Three of us swayed one early morning. I was in Sully's arms. Henry in my womb, awaiting his entry in the world. I understand there are amazing doctors who now encourage moms to dance in the delivery room to help ease contraction pains and ready the body, mind, and spirit for delivery.

Our dance felt right, even though it was likely time to head to the hospital since contractions had begun. I could push through the pain as we danced. I had not yet seen Henry eye-to-eye but had held him. We hold each other still.

Henry, thank you for being.

And now about incredible you...

Somewhere tonight a nurse is holding the hand of someone dying alone, an officer is consoling a grieving mother, a stranger is blanketing a malnourished soul with soup and conversation, a prosecutor is going over evidence and case law to put a predator in prison, and a defense attorney is working pro bono to release a wrongly convicted man. The hope is not in this all going away. The hope springs in the love coursing through tenderness, justice, and compassion.

And then there is wonderful you.

Your life may be in a solemn hour; maybe it's a witching hour of frustration, chaos, and concern.

Perhaps you have pressed pause on your dreams.

Perhaps you are hard on yourself, focused on the toughest things to do, not seeing how much you have already done.

I get it. I push myself ahead, forgetting to stop and put the plaque on the wall or smell the freshly mowed grass. My dad put everything on the wall. His life was visible, the grandeur palpable. There has to be a healthy line between overwhelmingly boasting and self-congratulating versus taking time to honor evidence of optimism.

Celebrate your victories. Do not let others determine what is worthy of praise. Celebrate goodness as you see it, so you'll remember when days grow dusty and discouraging.

My dear friend is a corporate attorney for an international entertainment company. We were talking recently about the laws around minors and protections designed for their safety. She affirmed, "We need to have adults in charge of the buttons."

You are blessed to be in charge of the buttons igniting your whole life.

You've got to flip the switch to view this power as a gift instead of burden.

Be intense and intent on the voracity and limitless capacity of your incredible power to conquer your dreams.

Every one of us is called for meaningful work. Not all of us are paid for the work, but there is immeasurable compensation now and later, far beyond our imagination.

Arm yourself with these anchors: I am. I can. I will.

I am able. No matter the obstacles, I am able to work hard, read, discover, grow, seek help, and serve. *I am* people know fails and falls are part of every life. Missteps and pain are temporary and not a vast conspiracy. A bad episode is not a bad life. *I am* people renew their passport at 90.

I can liberate my life. *I can* people know their vast worth, leaning into grit, grace, hope, and love, no matter the circumstance. *I can* people are optimists who believe there is a solution; perhaps it is simply time. Sure, you might be scared, enduring sleepless nights and sweaty palms as of late, but you can liberate yourself by charging forward with - and through - the fear. Stop the propulsion of perfection. You are a warrior even when you are at rest.

I will go. I will love, serve, rest, digest, and dive in. I will test limits—theirs and mine—doing so with integrity and fortitude. I will not let pressure swallow me, even when it envelopes me. Set off. Explore. *I will* people are inspired by insights and new directions.

Be light. Be the reminder of the enormous goodness in this world. And when you see the good in people and in their places and things - tell them. Stand amazed and humble. Share an awe. Imagine what life becomes when we see souls instead of bodies battling sags, globs, and imperfections.

Invincibility is a misperception. It is not flawless and fearless perfection. It is steadfast love.

Share this naked truth with your naked (authentic) self (even if your clothes are on):

Thank you for being.

We are easily broken by the unspoken.

Love more.

CHAPTER EIGHTEEN

SUMMATIONS, DECLARATIONS, AND THE EFFECTIVE MANAGEMENT OF ME

"This sucks!" is one of the best affirmations we ever receive. My soul sister friends are the first to claim it, while rallying one another to conquer.

"We love you. We've got this. It sucks."

Truth. Truth. Truth.

Life's trials necessitate burdens of proof and burdens of persuasion.

What else helps resuscitate a weary soul?

1. **Recognize the good.** As I write these very words a text has arrived with a request from a bathroom in my house. Do I give thanks for phones and extra toilet paper? The fact that the text didn't go to a group chat of non-family members *this time*? In everything, we can find a glint of light.

2. **React with what you want to receive.** Share an encouraging word, even it's to merely nudge yourself onward.

3. **Realize your power.** Commit to a good attitude 'here' even though you want to be 'there.' Surely you could write a country western song or poetic rap based on your present circumstance. Commence the lyrics now.

While attending my first yoga class, I thought I was masterfully holding a warrior pose until the instructor came by, tapped my shoulder, and whispered in my ear, "You ought to go back to child's pose." Have I mentioned how much I dislike yoga? I know we are all supposed to love it. I took the instructor's non-zen-like guidance and went into child's pose, noticing all the beautiful, tight people in front of me still donning a warrior stance. Sure, I wanted to leave or fall asleep. I wasn't enjoying myself and I wasn't good at it - yet.

In moments like this, don't look around for permission or affirmation before getting up and trying again. Get going. If you see others struggling, encourage them to rise.

No matter how precarious, lubberly or embarrassing, *may we all rise.*

Reflect. Rest. Recharge. These are the foundations for restoration.

Brave. Loving. Tired. Frustrated. You can be all of these, all at once. This is where cathartic wisdom and authentic beauty reside.

Be kind. Claim your worth.

*"I love non-judgmental friends who get me, and I can be
me. They see my quirkiness as funny, not fatal."*
- CECILY SULLIVAN

Whole living is communal. The interplay between us is what shapes us. Joy alights our communion, an intimate, shared understanding of worth and worthiness.

Have you ever yoked yourself to someone with low self-worth? Ever done so when they displayed high confidence or arrogance, with false courage, masking their true beliefs? They try to lift themselves by tearing you down, bit by bit or text by text.

You can break free with integrity.

Faith, a joyful perspective, and principled replies—this is a trinity for the whole of me. We build character, we fire up grit, grace, hope, and love when we decide to lead an abundant, robust, flourishing whole life.

What do you value? Is it the win at all cost or is it playing the game well? Both leave impact and imprints. What do you want your life to impart?

"To the best of my ability" is a presidential promise sworn on inauguration day. It should be part of our daily oath to be.

Shaken and wobbly? Do you understand how capable and awesome you are right now? Sure, there are ding-a-lings and cretins serving as CEOs, managers, PTA chairs, roommates, extended family members, gatekeepers, clinicians, and technicians, but they do not have to define what we believe and what we become. We ought to stop comparing our best and most with anyone else's effort. Be careful of where you seek approval and applause. Be your whole self in public and in private. There are billions of people on this earth; do not let one wreck your life. And be darn sure not to ruin anyone else. Take all of who you wonderfully are - the beautifully broken, shining, strong and struggling pieces - and use each part for a greater purpose beyond yourself.

There is power in the pause.

Light is togetherness - the alone *I* evolving to the sanctity of *we*.

"You can do this." These are words we do not always want to hear. Sometimes we just want to know someone understands the pain. Affirmation heals well before answers offering solutions. We need a balance of protection, understanding, listening, coaching, teaching, and steadfast presence.

Earnestly say,

"I'm so sorry you are going through such a hard time."

"I'm here."

"How can I help?"

Then pause.

Wait for the one hurting to share what they need, even if they do not know.

Get comfortable with "I don't know," although it is against the hype of search engines and unsolicited advice. Get comfortable in silence and the power of quiet presence.

"I don't know" is a sufficient, honest reply when testifying on a witness stand or when someone you love is holding your hand.

Kindness is the mark of the mighty.

"My marks and scars I carry with me
to be a witness."
– JOHN BUNYAN

Our son Henry carries scars most do not notice as they are on the inside of his arms. You and I carry our scars in various pockets and parts.

Henry is a prolific, insightful, and brave writer who directs his siblings in original scripted series. He says,

"We have to love every part of ourselves because when we do, we finally figure out that we are wonderfully made. All of it fits. I am not ashamed of worry. It's in middle school and it's in me. I can do amazing things with these feelings, observations, and odd cafeteria smells. If you don't like now, it's not forever. Dream of the next adventure, or in my case - movie to create, while you are stuck on the bus ride with a clogged toilet and people throwing stink bombs. I don't want to forget. I want to laugh while I conquer."

As I write, he has thrown a small ball and knocked down his sister's carefully crafted tower. I looked at him with a mother's silent query,

"What are you going to do about it?"

He said, "I'll fix what I broke."

He has, he does, he will—with grit, grace, hope, and love.

Henry knows what many easily forget, *kindness is courageous.*

The effective management of me.

What if you believed in all that is possible for your beautiful whole life?

What if we were all brave enough to believe in our awesome capacity?

Cake helps. During the last year of my dad's life, we could see his decline. Slowing, no longer a steady gait, days of confusion, and days of wisdom were part of dialysis for nine years. Learned behavior from life and football encouraged no wasted food, belonging to "the clean plate club," and also meant a life-long battle with weight. Illness and a myriad of maladies made weight a less pertinent issue. Dad loved cake and Mom decided toward the end he ought to have this treat every morning. For the last year of his life, on Sunday evenings Mom baked a sheet cake, cutting a piece for each day, wrapping it up to later heat and serve warm for breakfast. He loved every bite. He loved and adored her. We do not necessarily become what we behold. We become what we believe.

It was no longer time to fuss overeating the right thing, as soon my dad would have no appetite. Eat cake for breakfast. She offered. He obliged. This, in the midst of a long goodbye, is love.

You are created to love.

You are a creator of love.

We may lose our way to love through texts and emojis. They are cute, funny, and fast, and can become replacements for what we could say or what needs to be said and done. Be intentional and perceptive with love. A deliberate text can gird someone up to conquer a wilderness or worrisome test. Try these six words: Be brave. Be bold. Be light.

Or these three: You've got this!

Stop waiting on your glorious becoming. It doesn't matter if others don't get you. You are in charge of your whole life. Let the awesome unfold. Seek people and communities who enlighten, engage, love, and serve. Be with those who are true friends, even as new friends.

In *The Tiger Rising*, author Kate DiCamillo's main character, Rob Horton, is a sad, utterly alone sixth grader. Shortly after Rob's mother died, they moved from Jacksonville, Florida to the small town of Lister. There Rob is bullied, and even asked to leave school for a while because of horrible red marks covering his legs. Those marks are outward signs of Rob's inner pain. He tucks his feelings away, so he won't have to think about things.

Things like having a friend.

A potential friend appears in the form of a girl named Sistine. Rob discovers a real tiger in a cage in the woods and wants to share his encounter. This is scary. Not the tiger; the act of making himself vulnerable. In anxious breaths he tells her about his discovery. She doesn't berate him, discount him or demean him. She simply says, "Where?"

Who are the people in your life who would answer "*Where?*" when you share you know where a tiger resides?

We do not have to make ourselves vulnerable to those who may never fully see us.

To become whole, we thrive in a community of authentically bold grit, grace, hope, and love.

Walk into ambition in lieu of paring down dreams. Insist on loving yourself instead of dismissing who you truly are.

Wonderfully change one thing with relentless determination and the rest of your life will follow.

Others may not see or fully know you.

As a young associate in a labor and employment law firm, I was given an early chance to defend a corporate client in a deposition. The client was a franchise producing a popular calendar with girls in bikinis standing next to cars, boats, and arenas boasting a wink and a smile. I prepared weeks in advance, coming to the office on weekends, eschewing evenings out with friends to ready myself for testimony and questioning. The date came, the deposition went well, and the client was pleased. A partner called and said, "The client is so happy they delivered a present for you. I put it on your desk." Driving back to the office, feeling proud of the day, I envisioned what might await my arrival. On my desk, I didn't find cash, cake or a new briefcase. There to thank me was a note atop a bikini girl calendar, extra small t-shirt, cropped shorts, and a signed extra-large poster.

This was not the effective management of me.

Incentives work when we understand what motivates our team.

Some may see you before you see yourself.

When friends, new acquaintances or strangers do something kind, such as welcoming us into their home for a meal, making a stirring presentation or taking time to show us something or better still, show our kids, maybe share an experience bringing joy, or give us tickets to visit a museum we thought we would miss, I look at them and offer this tender declaration:

> "When you lie in bed tonight and wonder if you've done
> something wonderful today, the answer is 'Yes.'"

I am thankful.

Their presence has changed me. My life is better because of them.

I want them to know.

We all need to hear this, for caught in our self-centered doubt, worry, and exhaustion, we miss how small acts of merely being ourselves offer great meaning.

The world is not out to get you. The world awaits your wonder.

Award-winning actor Sterling K. Brown gave a poignant acceptance speech that stays with me. In it, he expressed his love for his children sharing, "Your daddy loves you with the strength of a thousand suns. I'll see you Monday after work."

Who do you love with the strength of a thousand suns?

Tell them, often.

Be the wonder.

CHAPTER NINETEEN

HOME

Sanctuary.

When things are stressful at our house, Sully will often say, "We need to do a better job of loving each other." Home is not a place where we should be coming to do battle every day. Home is a sanctuary. Not a place where there's a need to gear up for more battles within, it's the place we find reassurance and peace. The place where we renew and restore for battles beyond.

Home is with my family. When we are together, I can easily forget to let go and enjoy. Caught in my own head, I miss the bliss.

For some, going home is uninviting. It is not what we want. It brings anything but a hero's welcome.

The pull of home, a place of abiding in love's pure light, may not be where our feet currently reside. A journey, loved ones, nature, neighbors, a seat at the water's edge, a warm meal and bed—any one of these are home. The ache for home is a longing for wholeness.

We create home by living within the four walls of grit, grace, hope, and love.

Light will guide you home.

There were challenges to reuniting a nation beleaguered by Civil War. John Wilkes Booth heard President Abraham Lincoln's first declaration for voting rights for all men and hated this idea. He planned assassination based on rehearsals in Ford's Theatre. Today, tourists flood this historic place to see where Booth shot President Lincoln. Doing so in reverent observance and long lines, they may fail to cross the street and see where Lincoln drew his last breath. Petersen House, a boarding house across from Ford's Theatre, provided lodging, even shared beds and nooks for those needing rest. Doctors attending Lincoln and soldiers carrying him out of Ford's Theatre were audience members. There was no contingency plan. Soldiers had to draw swords just to make way into the street. Crowds in front of the theater were not dispersing but growing larger. It was a muddy, rainy evening offering little visibility. Old buildings tend to have high steps. Henry Safford, a boarder, heard the chaos outside Petersen House. With a view above street level, he stood on the steps outside the front door holding a lamp, yelling, "Bring him here!" The soldiers and doctors followed the light. They moved Lincoln to Petersen House, not thinking he could be saved, but to offer dignity to the dying president. They asked Safford to lead them to the closest clean bed. Safford took them to a room belonging to Willie Clark, another tenant.

A light in the darkness.

A call and a way.

Bring him here.

A boarder gave up his room, his bed, his rest. Safford, Clark and other tenants may have walked the streets all night as dignitaries and onlookers came to pay their respects.

Bring him here.

Bring him home.

This is who we are. This is what we do in times of crisis and calamity. Strangers bring light and hope in darkness. Life is robust, radiant, and temporal. There is tremendous good in the world, even in muddied chaos. With light, we guide each other home.

The rooms of Petersen House are as sacred as Ford's Theatre, for they are home to grit, grace, hope, and love.

Who calls you home?

To somebody *you are home*. They find freedom and refuge in you. This is a precious, sacred gift.

Heading home is going to a place where you already belong.

Wherever you find sanctuary, a space of confidence, rest, and restoration, the place where you unmask and are welcome, where they notice when you are gone, where grit, grace, hope, and love abide, you are home.

CHAPTER TWENTY

A BENEDICTION

Accept the miracle.

About two miles down the road, rests an old, well-worn house. It is my favorite home in Atlanta. It is nearly one hundred years old and every room has cracks in the ceiling and creaking, aching floors. I love every part of this house. I walk by and dream. An architect and designer would tell me each room requires major renovation. If I owned it, I would simply live it in for a bit, so we could get to know each other. The main grand staircase has a hand carved railing culminating with a large glass finial. It reminds me of Frank Capra's 1946 movie classic "It's a Wonderful Life" where George Bailey grabs the wooden staircase finial with distain when he hates his life and later cradles and kisses it that same evening after he learns to love his life.

It's said a glass or crystal finial was once a status symbol indicating a home was paid in full. How true to our humanness that we select something so fragile to symbolize finality and vitality.

My dad's been gone for many years. He wrote notes on books, scratch pads, and personal stationery. His poor handwriting leads to deciphering deliberate words written in a cryptic script.

On a recent difficult day, our daughter Cecily picked up an old Yardley soap container. She found it in a drawer in our dining room. She announced, "Mom, there's a note in here for you."

Inside the green painted metal case was soap, fragrantly filling me as I saw the backside of Dad's calling card. I love how he never called them business cards, for all his life whether as a pastor, business leader, husband, dad, friend, or messing up, sad, wandering, joyful, eating too much, asking too much, dreaming hugely, and feeling deeply, he responded to the call to love.

A calling to love.

A note of love from him filled with wonderful words of life.

He is gone. Love lingers.

How amazing my daughter, who never met my dad, found this gift waiting for me.

Someone needs a note from you today. A life will change because of your encouragement.

There is a love note waiting for you each day.

It says,

> *Dear friend,*
> *You are so loved.*
> *You are uniquely, wonderfully made.*
> *Go. Serve. Carry others. Save some for the other guy.*
> *Alight life. Don't be ashamed or afraid of tears, anger,*
> *and exhaustion. Acknowledge the pain; put it to work.*
> *Strengthen people with truth, laughter, and compassion.*
> *Seek more life together.*
> *Astonish the world with grit, grace, hope, and love. Don't*

get caught up in lies or languish long in lament. Figure out
what you are good at, what you love, and how combining
those forces will help people. Use your gifts to expel cruelty
and suffering. Your story will not end in ashes when you
are courageously kind.
Celebrate the good. Work hard. Rest. Embrace outrageous
dreams.
Build your bridge.
Recognize illness. Get help before it overtakes and robs
joy. Be open to life being far better than you imagined,
even when it is hard and lonely. Remember, you are not
alone when you are crushed in spirit. Miracles abound
in the mistakes, misfortune, and mess. Life, family, a
home, meal, job, or friends don't have to be perfect to be
wonderful.
Onward, brave one.
With love,
Me

Let these truths linger.

Do not confuse visibility with value.

If you long to grasp glory, grow in grit, grace, hope, and love.

You can do this.

You are incredibly armed and able.

Go.

Together, let us begin.

RECOGNITIONS AND GRATITUDE

For every person who breathes life into someone else's dream, you are the love of a thousand suns.

Family and friends, your grit, grace, hope and love make everything possible.

For all those who nurtured, encouraged, inspired, and fostered this book into publication and distribution, I am tenderly thankful. Your name, even if not printed in this book, is written on my heart. You are radiant goodness in this world.

In life, the only thing that matters is faith expressing itself though love. Soul sisters, warrior friends, Beautifully Broken community, editors (Alice Eachus, Paula Fisher, Celeste Johnston, Mia Dunkle, and Susan Carroll), Stephanie Husk and the entire Deep Blue Insight team, Carmen Miller, Ryan Sprenger, Jaye Watson, Kenny Hamilton, Amy Dickie, Elizabeth Searcy, Stephen Weinstein, Holly Proctor, Rebecca

Nixon, Nanette Nicholson, Rena Kilgannon, Jennifer Johnson, Bobby Pearce, Pat Sibley, LaKeicia Denson, Jo Reeves, Steve Yee, Chris Sodeman, Chevy Arnold, Cinda Boomershine, Mark Boomershine, Hope Cohn, John Schneider, Brad Pope, Melanie Pope, Shea Fleming, Allyson Maske, Joe Williams, Alicia Batchelor, Scott Batchelor, Cliff Willimon, The Schenck School, The Speech School, Ivan Luengas, Judy Luengas, Cia Cummings, Goonie Moms, judges, attorneys and co-counsel, IEP/504 and special education advocates, teachers, More Than Sparrows, Twelve, Sully Christmas Wine Tasters, book clubs, Children's Healthcare of Atlanta (CHOA), Children's Miracle Network hospitals, Atlanta Police Department, Atlanta Fire Rescue Department, and all of you bridge builders and brave beloveds who take on the heavy yokes—you are magnificent, splendid lights. Your lives feed and fill. You show up and ignite the wonderful. Oh, to grow old together while we are still young. Young is right now, whatever our age, for we are plucky and ready to dance or belt out a song. Let's hold this same vigor at fifty, eighty, ninety, and beyond.

Sully and our four wonders, you are my world and a world lives in us. Elizabeth Barrett Browning said of love, "you're something between a miracle and a dream." How glorious to live in this holy space. Mess, stress, frustrations, the hard, and beautiful—we've got this. Jack, Henry, Cecily, and Gabrielle Joy, I'm glad we spoke about each story in this book. As you grow older, you may be tempted to count how many times each one of you is referenced. No order or number will ever fully capture my love for you. I could never fill one book or even a lifetime of literature with the love and joy you bring. These stories are merely threads in a grand, magnificent tapestry. Remember the spot I point to on my heart that is just for you. No object or being will ever fill your sacred place. As you grow and begin your own families, my heart and spaces there will grow, too. For your whole life and far beyond, your dad and I will love you. Long after we are gone, you will still have each other. Your deep, abiding friendships are miraculous riches to have and to hold.

In fact, for all of us in this world, within and beyond blood lines, deep, abiding friendships are astounding treasures of our whole lives, for they are home and they are love.

May we continue to grow in grit, grace, hope, and love.

You, my friend, are already worthy of their astounding reward.

ADDITIONAL RESOURCES

Chapter One: A Privilege And An Adventure

Cat Rescued After Being Stuck on a Pole for Three Days. Written by Joe Tacopino. The New York Post. Posted March 23, 2018. https://nypost.com/2018/03/26/cat-rescued-after-being-stuck-on-pole-for-three-days/
Ruth 1:16
Luke 10:25-37
Amazing Grace. Lyrics by John Newton.

Chapter Two: Kaleidoscope

Central Washington Offers The Ultimate Act Of Sportsmanship. Written by Graham Hays. espnW.com. Posted April 28, 2008.
Six *Years Later, Integrity Wins Again.* Written by Graham Hays. espnW.com. Posted April 28, 2014.
Peterson, Eugene H. *The Message.* www.Bible Gateway.com. 4 April 2018.

Chapter Three: Yet I

Judge's Unbelievable Compassion for a Veteran. Written by Billy Kirby, Jr. The Fayetteville Observer. Posted April 19, 2016. https://www.fayobserver.com/article/20160419/News/304199858

Chapter Four: Beautifully Broken

Senator Robert F. Kennedy, Indianapolis, Indiana. April 4, 1968, speech given after the assignation of Martin Luther King, Jr. https://www.jfklibrary.org/Research/Research-Aids/Ready-Reference/RFK-Speeches/Statement-on-the-Assassination-of-Martin-Luther-King.aspx
Read and listen to Senator Kennedy's full speech in Indianapolis as well as other powerful proclamations found at www.jfklibrary.org.
Welcome to Dysfunction Junction.
Music and lyrics by Sarah Crossman Sullivan.

Chapter Five: Our Dwelling Place
Chapter Six: Grit

Duckworth, Angela, *Grit: The Power of Passion and Perseverance.* New York: Simon & Schuster, 2016.
Gladwell, Malcom, *Outliers.* New York: Little, Brown and Company, Back Bay Books, 2011.

Chapter Seven: Resilience

Angelou, Maya, *I Know Why The Caged Bird Sings.* New York: Random House, 1969.
A Guide to Promoting Resilience in Children: Strengthening the Human Spirit. Written by Edith H. Grotberg, PhD.,
The Hague: Bernard van Leer Foundation. Copyright 1995. All rights reserved. Used by permission. ISBN 90-6195-038-4. ISSN 1382-4813.
Examples of dyslexia resources:
Madebydyslexia.org (The World is Made by Dyslexia
The Yale Center for Dyslexia and Creativity, http://dyslexia.yale.edu/snapshots.php#

Q&A: The Unappreciated Benefits of Dyslexia. Written by Danielle Venton. Wired. Posted September 20, 2011. https://www.wired.com/2011/09/dyslexic-advantage/

Schenck.org

Atlantaspeechschool.org

Harvard Smithsonian Center for Astrophysics, https://www.cfa.harvard.edu/dyslexia/LVL/*E Is For Empathy: Sesame Workshop Takes A Crack At Kindness.* Written by Cory Turner, National Public Radio, nprED, October 17, 2016. Also shared on NPR—Morning Edition. https://www.npr.org/sections/ed/2016/10/17/497827991/a-sesame-study-in-kindness

Chapter Eight: Courage

'Fearless Girl' Statue Stares Down Wallstreet's Iconic Bull. Written by Verena Dobnik. Associated Press. Posted March 8, 2017. https://www.washington-times.com/news/2017/mar/8/fearless-girl-statue-stares-down-wall-streets-icon/

'Charging Bull' Sculptor Says 'Fearless Girl' Distorts His Art. He's Fighting Back. Written by Katie Mettler. The Washington Post. Posted April 12, 2017. https://www.washingtonpost.com/news/morning-mix/wp/2017/04/12/charging-bull-sculptor-says-fearless-girl-distorts-his-art-hes-fighting-back/?noredirect=on&utm_term=.628654f496b0

Wall Street's Fearless Girl Statue Gets A New Place Of Honor. Written by Karen Matthews, Associated Press. Posted December 10, 2018. https://www.usnews.com/news/business/articles/2018-12-10/fearless-girl-statue-gets-new-perma-nent-home

In choosing our dog's middle name we understood "Batman" is a trademark and brand of DC COMICS and our children selected the name to honor the DC COMICS trademark and brand. Reagan Batman Sullivan has since passed away.

Chapter Nine: Grace

Research on Pearl Harbor included oral family histories, recordings, photographs, and reports provided by Amy Shepherd Dickie, Mary Kidd Plumer, Christopher M. Sullivan, and Marcia Isom Henry. Additional resources are available at https://www.nps.gov/valr/index.htm

Chapter Ten: Believe
Chapter Eleven: Becoming

Alaska Bird Makes Longest Nonstop Flight Ever Measured. Written by Dave Hansford, National Geographic News, September 14, 2007. https://www.nationalgeographic.com/animals/2007/09/alaska-bird-longest-mirgation/
Thwarting Metastasis by Breaking Cancer's Legs with Gold Rods. Written by Ben Brumfield. www.news.gatech.ed. Posted June 26, 2017. http://www.rh.gatech.edu/news/592976/thwarting-metastasis-breaking-cancers-legs-gold-rods

Chapter Twelve: Hope

Sendak, Maurice. *Where the Wild Things Are.* New York: Harper Collins, 1988.
Coach Bobby Knight On Why He Is So Unpleasant. Interview with Coach Bobby Knight by Andrew Goldman, The New York Times Magazine, March 1, 2013. Posted March 3, 2013. https://www.nytimes.com/2013/03/03/magazine/coach-bobby-knight-on-why-hes-so-unpleasant.html
For more information on Ashley's Sack, currently on display at National Museum of African American History and Culture, see https://nmaahc.si.edu
The Forgotten Plague: Tuberculosis in America. The American Experience. Airing on PBS on February 10, 2015. All rights reserved. Used by permission. http://www.pbs.org/wgbh/americanexperience/films/plague/

Chapter Thirteen: Light & Darkness

Hurt, performed by Nine Inch Nails and later, Johnny Cash. Written by Trent Reznor.
Music Video featuring Johnny Cash and June Carter Cash, produced by Rick Rubin and directed by Mark Romanek.
Upside-Rainbows: The Science Behind Circumzenithal and Circumhorizontal Arcs. Written by Jon Erdman. Weather.com. Posted July 30, 2014. https://weather.com/science/news/upside-down-rainbows-circumzenithal-circumhorizontal-arcs-20140730
What Are Sun Halos? Written by Chrissy Warrilow. Weather.com. Posted June 26, 2014. https://weather.com/news/news/sun-halos-florida-20140416

Chapter Fourteen: Love

A Female Viking Warrior Confirmed By Genomics. Charlotte Hedenstierna-Jonson, Anna Kjellström, Torun Zachrisson, Maja Krzewińska, Veronica Sobrado, Neil Price, Torsten Günther, Mattias Jakobsson, Anders Götherström, and Jan Storå. American Journal of Physical Anthropology. First published: September 8, 2017. https://doi.org/10.1002/ajpa.23308
Hero Monkey Helped Lost Man Survive For Days In The Amazon. Written by Lia Eustachewich. New York Post. Posted March 24, 2017. https://nypost.com/2017/03/24/hero-monkeys-helped-lost-man-survive-for-days-in-the-amazon/
Growing Up Maya Angelou. Written by Lucinda Moore, Smithsonian Magazine, April 2003. All rights reserved. Used by permission. https://www.smithsonianmag.com/arts-culture/growing-up-maya-angelou-79582387/

Chapter Fifteen: Build Your Bridge
Chapter Sixteen: Shush

"Captain America" is a brand and trademark owned by Marvel Characters, Inc.

You Are Strong. Interview With Chris Evans: Chris Evans' Advice For People With Anxiety and Depression.

You Tube Channel: Motivation Madness. https://www.youtube.com/watch?v=HqSoxMOrVeE

See also: Chris Evans' Tweet on January 13, 2018—"For anyone struggling w anxiety. Here's some advice I got a long time ago." https://t.co/w57xle7qDU" @ChrisEvans

Chapter Seventeen: Thank You For Being
Chapter Eighteen: Summations, Declarations, And The Effective Management of Me

DiCamillo, Kate, *The Tiger Rising*. Massachusetts: Candlewick Press, 2006. pp. 3-4; 41-42.

THE TIGER RISING. Copyright © 2001 by Kate DiCamillo Reproduced by permission of the publisher, Candlewick Press, Somerville, MA.

Chapter Nineteen: Home

For more information on The Peterson House, see https://www.nps.gov/foth/the-petersen-house.htm

**Capture the strength of growing
in grit, grace, hope & love.
Rejuvenate communities, companies, and lives.**

Go to www.SarahCrossmanSullivan.com to sign-up for exceptional opportunities to nourish, revive, and thrive:

- **Speaking engagements and performance coaching**—Sarah brings unique, fresh captivating motivation and readily implementable restoration for corporations, teams, schools, and non-profit organizations.
- **Leadership guides**—bring Beautifully Broken & Astoundingly Whole principles to your department, group, family, and friends.
- **Small group materials** - share ways for diving deeper into how love radically, powerfully transforms how we lead and live.
- **Inspiring newsletters, podcasts, and posts**—go to www.SarahCrossmanSullivan.com and follow @SarahCrossmanSullivan on Twitter, Instagram, LinkedIn and Facebook.

*Love, or the absence of it, is at the core of everything.
Let's radically love more and wonderfully
change the world.*
- SARAH CROSSMAN SULLIVAN, JD

SARAH CROSSMAN SULLIVAN, JD, is a successful attorney-counselor-advocate, writer, speaker, and corporate consultant. She revitalizes individual and corporate performance by awakening love-driven leadership. She has spent more than twenty years serving as an employment lawyer, Assistant District Attorney, chief corporate counsel, entrepreneur, and special education expert. Featured on a variety of major news outlets, Sarah is an in-demand speaker, known for her dynamic, invigorating style and humble, funny, relatable stories on life – from work to friendships to parenting and marriage. She helps people conquer dreams while embracing the mess, mundane, and marvelous. She lives in Atlanta, Georgia with her husband, Chris, four children, and two dogs.

Connect with Sarah for corporate and non-profit speaking engagements or to simply find shared inspiration, encouragement, and joy.

www.SarahCrossmanSullivan.com
⊙ 🛇 🅕 🅨 🅲 **/@SarahCrossmanSullivan**